Modern Critical Interpretations

Jane Austen's
Mansfield Park

Modern Critical Interpretations

These and other titles in preparation

Modern Critical Interpretations

Jane Austen's
Mansfield Park

Edited and with an introduction by

Harold Bloom
Sterling Professor of the Humanities
Yale University

Chelsea House Publishers ◇ *1987*
NEW YORK ◇ NEW HAVEN ◇ PHILADELPHIA

© 1987 by Chelsea House Publishers, a division of Chelsea
House Educational Communications, Inc.
  133 Christopher Street, New York, NY 10014
  345 Whitney Avenue, New Haven, CT 06511
  5014 West Chester Pike, Edgemont, PA 19028

Introduction © 1987 by Harold Bloom

Printed and bound in the United States of America

∞ The paper used in this publication meets the minimum
requirements of the American National Standard for
Permanence of Paper for Printed Library Materials,
Z39.48–1984.

Library of Congress Cataloging-in-Publication Data
Jane Austen's Mansfield Park.
    (Modern critical interpretations)
    Bibliography: p.
    Includes index.
    Summary: A collection of eight critical essays on Jane
Austen's novel "Mansfield Park" arranged in chronological
order of publication.
    1. Austen, Jane, 1775–1817. Mansfield Park.
[1. Austen, Jane, 1775–1817. Mansfield Park.
2.   English literature—History and criticism]   I. Bloom,
Harold.   II. Series.
PR4034.M33J36   1987   823'.7   86-12990
ISBN 0-87754-944-3 (alk. paper)

Contents

Editor's Note

This book gathers together a representative selection of what I judge to be the best criticism of Jane Austen's novel *Mansfield Park,* arranged in the chronological order of its original publication. I am grateful to Susan Laity for her erudition and judgment in helping to edit this volume.

The editor's introduction centers upon Fanny Price as an inheritor of the Protestant will, and traces an analogue to Wordsworthian concerns in her devoted need to carry the past spirit of Mansfield Park alive into its present and its future. Thomas R. Edwards begins the chronological sequence of criticism with a meditation upon the novel's difficult moral beauty, its ironic choice of integrity over liveliness of spirit. This is akin to Alistair M. Duckworth's analysis of the Crawfords' schemes for "the improvement of the estate," which would dissolve the crucial metaphors for the "organic" societal values in which Fanny Price and Jane Austen believe.

Stuart M. Tave, exploring the problem of the propriety of the amateur theatricals in *Mansfield Park,* helps current readers to see how subtly correct Fanny's moral judgment proves to be in this teapot tempest, as it may now seem to uninstructed readers. A parallel difficulty in Austen's ironic art is expounded by Juliet McMaster, who shows precisely how decorous, polite conversation in *Mansfield Park* can be linked to really intense and powerful emotions, negative and positive. The novel's greatest difficulty, the enigma of Fanny Price's evident weakness and humility coexisting with her moral strength and pride, is handsomely studied by Susan Morgan, in what seems to me the most enlightening essay yet written upon *Mansfield Park,* and upon its conviction that "what is evil is to mistake style for substance, forms of understanding for truth, fictions for reality."

The novel's social vision is examined by David Monaghan, who shrewdly notes that Austen's implicit thesis links charm and social influence. Nina Auerbach, rather more flamboyantly, sees Fanny Price as "a Romantic monster," Jane Austen's answer to Byron's Childe Harold. In this book's final essay, Margaret Kirkham returns us to Austen's ironic vision, which she judges to be a feminist irony directed against us as readers. Doubtless another critical age will arise that shall reorient Austen's ironies yet again, but that is (or will be) one more tribute to the subtlest and most artistic master of irony in the English novel.

Introduction

I

The oddest yet by no means inapt analogy to Jane Austen's art of representation is Shakespeare's—oddest, because she is so careful of limits, as
classical as Ben Jonson in that regard, and Shakespeare transcends all limits.
Austen's humor, her mode of rhetorical irony, is not particularly Shakespearean, and yet her precision and accuracy of representation is. Like
Shakespeare, she gives us figures, major and minor, utterly consistent each
in her or his own mode of speech and being, and utterly different from
one another. Her heroines have firm selves, each molded with an individ-
uality that continues to suggest Austen's reserve of power, her potential
for creating an endless diversity. To recur to the metaphor of oddness, the
highly deliberate limitation of social scale in Austen seems a paradoxical
theater of mind in which so fecund a humanity could be fostered. Irony,
the concern of most critics of Austen, seems more than a trope in her work,
seems indeed to be the condition of her language, yet hardly accounts for
the effect of moral and spiritual power that she so constantly conveys,
however implicitly or obliquely.

Ian Watt, in his permanently useful *The Rise of the Novel,* portrays
Austen as Fanny Burney's direct heir in the difficult art of combining the
rival modes of Samuel Richardson and Henry Fielding. Like Burney, Austen
is thus seen as following the Richardson of *Sir Charles Grandison* in a "minute
presentation of daily life," while emulating Fielding "in adopting a more
detached attitude to her narrative material, and in evaluating it from a comic
and objective point of view." Watt goes further when he points out that
Austen tells her stories in a discreet variant of Fielding's manner "as a
confessed author," though her ironical juxtapositions are made to appear
not those of "an intrusive author but rather of some august and impersonal
spirit of social and psychological understanding."

1

And yet, as Watt knows, Austen truly is the daughter of Richardson, and not of Fielding, just as she is the ancestor of George Eliot and Henry James, rather than of Dickens and Thackeray. Her inwardness is an ironic revision of Richardson's extraordinary conversion of English Protestant sensibility into the figure of Clarissa Harlowe, and her own moral and spiritual concerns fuse in the crucial need of her heroines to sustain their individual integrities, a need so intense that it compels them to fall into those errors about life that are necessary for life (to adopt a Nietzschean formulation). In this too they follow, though in a comic register, the pattern of their tragic precursor, the magnificent but sublimely flawed Clarissa Harlowe.

Richardson's *Clarissa*, perhaps still the longest novel in the language, seems to me also still the greatest, despite the achievements of Austen, Dickens, George Eliot, Henry James, and Joyce. Austen's Elizabeth Bennet and Emma Woodhouse, Eliot's Dorothea Brooke and Gwendolen Harleth, James's Isabel Archer and Milly Theale—though all these are Clarissa Harlowe's direct descendants, they are not proportioned to her more sublime scale. David Copperfield and Leopold Bloom have her completeness; indeed Joyce's Bloom may be the most complete representation of a human being in all of literature. But they belong to the secular age; Clarissa Harlowe is poised upon the threshold that leads from the Protestant religion to a purely secular sainthood.

C. S. Lewis, who read Milton as though that fiercest of Protestant temperaments had been an orthodox Anglican, also seems to have read Jane Austen by listening for her echoings of the New Testament. Quite explicitly, Lewis named Austen as the daughter of Dr. Samuel Johnson, greatest of literary critics and rigorous Christian moralist:

> I feel . . . sure that she is the daughter of Dr. Johnson: she inherits
> his commonsense, his morality, even much of his style.

The Johnson of *Rasselas* and of *The Rambler,* surely the essential Johnson, is something of a classical ironist, but we do not read Johnson for his ironies, or for his dramatic representations of fictive selves. Rather we read him as we read Koheleth; he writes wisdom literature. That Jane Austen is a wise writer is indisputable, but we do not read *Pride and Prejudice* as though it were Ecclesiastes. Doubtless, Austen's religious ideas were as profound as Samuel Richardson's were shallow, but *Emma* and *Clarissa* are Protestant novels without being in any way religious. What is most original about the representation of Clarissa Harlowe is the magnificent intensity of her slowly described dying, which goes on for about the last third of

Richardson's vast novel, in a Puritan ritual that celebrates the preternatural strength of her will. For that is Richardson's sublime concern: the self-reliant apotheosis of the Protestant will. What is tragedy in *Clarissa* becomes serious or moral comedy in *Pride and Prejudice* and *Emma,* and something just the other side of comedy in *Mansfield Park* and *Persuasion.*

II

John Locke argues against personifying the will: persons can be free, but not the will, since the will cannot be constrained, except externally. While one sleeps, if someone moved one into another room and locked the door, and there one found a friend one wished to see, still one could not say that one was free thus to see whom one wished. And yet, Locke implies, the process of association does work as though the will were internally constrained. Association, in Locke's sense, is a blind substitution for reasoning, yet is within a reasoning process, though also imbued with affect. The mind, in association, is carried unwillingly from one thought to another, by accident as it were. Each thought appears, and carries along with it a crowd of unwanted guests, inhabitants of a room where thought would rather be alone. Association, on this view, is what the will most needs to be defended against.

Fanny Price, in *Mansfield Park,* might be considered a codescendant, together with Locke's association-menaced will, of the English Protestant emphasis upon the will's autonomy. Fanny, another precursor of the Virginia Woolf in *A Room of One's Own,* was shrewdly described by Lionel Trilling as "overtly virtuous and consciously virtuous," and therefore almost impossible to like, though Trilling (like Austen) liked Fanny very much. C. S. Lewis, though an orthodox moralist, thought Fanny insipid: "But into Fanny, Jane Austen, to counterbalance her apparent insignificance, has put really nothing except rectitude of mind; neither passion, nor physical courage, nor wit, nor resource." Nothing, I would say, except the Protestant will, resisting the powers of association and asserting its very own persistence, its own sincere intensity, and its own isolate sanctions. Trilling secularized these as "the sanctions of principle" and saw *Mansfield Park* as a novel that "discovers in principle the path to the wholeness of the self which is peace." That is movingly said, but secularization, in literature, is always a failed trope, since the distinction between sacred and secular is not actually a literary but rather a societal or political distinction. *Mansfield Park* is not less Protestant than *Paradise Lost,* even though Austen, *as a writer,* was as much a sect of one as John Milton was.

Fanny Price, like the Lockean will, fights against accident, against the crowding out of life by associations that are pragmatically insincere not because they are random, but because they are irrelevant, since whatever is not the will's own is irrelevant to it. If Fanny herself is an irony it is as Austen's allegory of her own defense against influences, human and literary, whether in her family circle, or in the literary family of Fanny Burney, Fielding, and Richardson. Stuart M. Tave shrewdly remarks that: "*Mansfield Park* is a novel in which many characters are engaged in trying to establish influence over the minds and lives of others, often in a contest or struggle for control." Fanny, as a will struggling only to be itself, becomes at last the spiritual center of Mansfield Park precisely because she has never sought power over any other will. It is the lesson of the Protestant will, whether in Locke or Austen, Richardson or George Eliot, that the refusal to seek power over other wills is what opens the inward eye of vision. Such a lesson, which we seek in Wordsworth and in Ruskin, is offered more subtly (though less sublimely) by Austen. Fanny, Austen's truest surrogate, has a vision of what Mansfield Park is and ought to be, which means a vision also of what Sir Thomas Bertram is or ought to be. Her vision is necessarily moral, but could as truly be called spiritual, or even aesthetic.

Perhaps that is why Fanny is not only redeemed but can redeem others. The quietest and most mundane of visionaries, she remains also one of the firmest: her dedication is to the future of Mansfield Park as the idea of order it once seemed to her. Jane Austen may not be a Romantic in the high Shelleyan mode, but Fanny Price has profound affinities with Wordsworth, so that it is no accident that *Mansfield Park* is exactly contemporary with *The Excursion*. Wordsworthian continuity, the strength that carries the past alive into the present, is the program of renovation that Fanny's pure will brings to Mansfield Park, and it is a program more Romantic than Augustan, so that Fanny's will begins to shade into the Wordsworthian account of the imagination. Fanny's exile to Portsmouth is so painful to her not for reasons turning upon social distinctions, but for causes related to the quiet that Wordsworth located in the bliss of solitude, or Virginia Woolf in a room of one's own:

> Such was the home which was to put Mansfield out of her head, and teach her to think of her cousin Edmund with moderated feelings. On the contrary, she could think of nothing but Mansfield, its beloved inmates, its happy ways. Everything where she now was was in full contrast to it. The elegance, propriety, regularity, harmony, and perhaps, above all, the peace and tran-

quility of Mansfield, were brought to her remembrance every hour of the day, by the prevalence of everything opposite to them *here*.

The living in incessant noise was, to a frame and temper delicate and nervous like Fanny's, an evil which no super-added elegance or harmony could have entirely atoned for. It was the greatest misery of all. At Mansfield, no sounds of contention, no raised voice, no abrupt bursts, no tread of violence, was ever heard; all proceeded in a regular course of cheerful orderliness; everybody had their due importance; everybody's feelings were consulted. If tenderness could be ever supposed wanting, good sense and good breeding supplied its place; and as to the little irritations, sometimes introduced by Aunt Norris, they were short, they were trifling, they were as a drop of water to the ocean, compared with the ceaseless tumult of her present abode. Here, everybody was noisy, every voice was loud (excepting, perhaps, her mother's, which resembled the soft monotony of Lady Bertram's, only worn into fretfulness). Whatever was wanted was halloo'd for, and the servants halloo'd out their excuses from the kitchen. The doors were in constant banging, the stairs were never at rest, nothing was done without a clatter, nobody sat still, and nobody could command attention when they spoke.

In a review of the two houses, as they appeared to her before the end of a week, Fanny was tempted to apply to them Dr. Johnson's celebrated judgment as to matrimony and celibacy, and say, that though Mansfield Park might have some pains, Portsmouth could have no pleasures.

The citation of Dr. Johnson's aphorism, though placed here with superb wit, transcends irony. Austen rather seeks to confirm, however implicitly, Johnson's powerful warning, in *The Rambler*, number 4, against the overwhelming realism of Fielding and Smollett (though their popular prevalence is merely hinted):

But if the power of example is so great, as to take possession of the memory by a kind of violence, and produce effects almost without the intervention of the will, care ought to be taken, that, when the choice is unrestrained, the best examples only should be exhibited; and that which is likely to operate so strongly, should not be mischievous or uncertain in its effects.

Fanny Price, rather more that Jane Austen perhaps, really does favor a Johnsonian aesthetic, in life as in literature. Portsmouth belongs to representation as practiced by Smollett, belongs to the cosmos of *Roderick Random*. Fanny, in willing to get back to Mansfield Park, and to get Mansfield Park back to itself, is willing herself also to renovate the world of her creator, the vision of Jane Austen that is *Mansfield Park*.

The Difficult Beauty of *Mansfield Park*

Thomas R. Edwards

From the Reverend James Stanier Clarke on, there have been those who
see no problem in *Mansfield Park;* it is a pleasing tale of virtue rewarded,
and this is enough. But such readers are happily rarer today than a hundred
years ago; some of our best critical minds have boggled at accepting Fanny
Price and Jane Austen's endorsement of her, and the novel's difficulties have
to be faced. Even its admirers have had to season their praise—often for
"technical" successes—with uneasy confessions that its moral frame may
be simpler than the fictional life it controls and judges. Only Lionel Trilling
observes that such uneasiness marks the prime virtue of the novel, whose
greatness is "commensurate with its power to offend." One learns more
about *Mansfield Park* from Mr. Trilling than from anyone else; but while I
share his belief in its greatness, I must confess some doubts about his way
of reading it. Although Fanny is indeed conceived ironically, I think Jane
Austen likes her and wants us to like her too—and despite Mr. Trilling's
invocation of "the shade of Pamela," I find it quite possible to do so. Nor
can I accept his view of Henry and Mary Crawford; surely they are presented consistently, and with entire persuasiveness, as being more gravely
flawed and less charming than he finds them, even at first reading; and in
Mary, especially, Jane Austen diagnoses a moral disorder that, because less
under conscious control, is both more alarming and more pitiful than the
deliberate insincerities and impersonations with which he charges them. In
short, Mr. Trilling concedes too much to the opposition, even to the extent

From *Nineteenth-Century Fiction* 20, no. 1 (June 1965). © 1965 by the Regents of
the University of California. The University of California Press, 1965.

of accepting the idea that the novel's praise "is not for social freedom but for social stasis," that it rejects "spiritness, vivacity, celerity, and lightness . . . as having nothing to do with virtue and happiness." Fanny and Edmund do reject freedom and vivacity, to be sure, and they are right to do so, considering who they are, but Jane Austen's view of the rejection is considerably more complicated and troubled than theirs. *Mansfield Park* does speak, as Mr. Trilling says, "to our secret inexpressible hopes" of escaping the "demands of personality" and secular complexity, but it warns as well that such an escape would cost us dearly.

It is first of all a singularly "beautiful" novel, one in which Jane Austen draws more than usual upon "scenic" resources. We attend more to where people are and what they are doing, and, more important, scene makes fuller contact with moral meaning. The excursion to Sotherton reveals this mingling of scene and meaning at its fullest. In contravention of Mrs. Norris's plans for organized sightseeing,

> the young people, meeting with an outward door, temptingly open on a flight of steps which led immediately to turf and shrubs, and all the sweets of pleasure-grounds, as by one impulse, one wish for air and liberty, all walked out.

The tangled syntax reflects another entanglement, of motive and evaluation, which the setting expresses too: it is good to thwart Mrs. Norris and all *calculations* about pleasure, yet the "impulse" seems too easily satisfied, the "sweets" too "immediate." (Are not gardens "tempting" places?) Guests should wait for invitations, but more than good manners seems at issue. There follows a dance-like movement through the landscape of lawn, Wilderness, and park, in which personal groupings, and the romantic possibilities they imply, dissolve and reform; Henry and Maria slip into the locked park, jealously followed by Julia and Rushworth; Mary and Edmund rejoin a lonely Fanny and are welcomed back by Authority in an amusingly theatrical tableau: "on [their] reaching the bottom of the steps to the terrace, Mrs. Rushworth and Mrs. Norris presented themselves at the top."

Happily, it is not the novelist but the characters who seek to exploit the scene's obvious symbolic possibilities. Mary, for one, has a lively sense of what might be done with the landscape:

> "We have taken such a very serpentine course; and the wood itself must be half a mile long in a straight line, for we have never seen the end of it yet, since we left the first great path.
>
> "But if you remember, before we left that first great path, we

saw directly to the end of it. We looked down the whole vista, and saw it closed by iron gates, and it could not have been more than a furlong in length."

"Oh! I know nothing of your furlongs, but I am sure it is a very long wood; and that we have been winding in and out ever since we came. . . ."

"We have been exactly a quarter of an hour here," said Edmund, taking out his watch. "Do you think we are walking four miles an hour?"

"Oh! do not attack me with your watch. A watch is always too fast or too slow. I cannot be dictated to by a watch."

Mary wants the Wilderness to be a Forest of Love (or at least Dalliance); her terms—serpentine course, first great path, not seeing to the end of it—playfully hint at an allegory of possible emotional involvement. She aims at a charming "femininity," but her projection of the scene as a Spenserian forest where time and space are suspended seems strained and coy. If Edmund (as so often) misses the point with his blundering addition of the iron gates and his inept insistence on furlongs and watches, we must still agree that time and space do exist, both as they affect people (Fanny is tired) and in their resonances as moral metaphors—to romanticize like this is to risk losing your bearings.

The danger becomes clear when Henry and Maria stand foiled by the gate:

"Your prospects, however, are too fair to justify want of spirits. You have a very smiling scene before you."

"Do you mean literally or figuratively? Literally I conclude. Yes, certainly, the sun shines and the park looks very cheerful. But unluckily that iron gate, that ha-ha, gives me a feeling of restraint and hardship. I cannot get out, as the starling said." As she spoke, and it was with expression, she walked to the gate; he followed her. "Mr. Rushworth is so long fetching this key!"

"And for the world you would not get out without the key and without Mr. Rushworth's authority and protection, or I think you might with little difficulty pass round the edge of the gate, here, with my assistance; I think it might be done, if you really wished to be more at large, and could allow yourself to think it not prohibited."

"Prohibited! nonsense! I certainly can get out that way, and I will."

This innuendo-ridden talk is what Edmund's stolid belief in time and space unwittingly saved him from. Jane Austen predicts the final disaster of Maria and Henry, but the moment evokes views of obligation and licence that are more than aspects of "plot" or "character." Freedom is tempting *because* it may be wicked. Each—Henry slyly, Maria impetuously—uses the setting to mirror improper interest in the other; since neither admits that the conversation is "figurative," they can dally with perfect efficiency (for both, getting into the park easily becomes "getting *out*") without taking any responsibility for their insinuations. People who imply that they mean more than they say, yet refuse to say what they mean, are both irritating and dishonest, and Fanny, though as usual she can't quite say it, senses thoroughly what is at stake: "you will certainly hurt yourself against those spikes—you will tear your gown—you will be in danger of slipping into the ha-ha. You had better not go." Setting becomes the image of moral violence.

The whole episode is beautifully drawn, but like other great moments in *Mansfield Park* it represents more than a local triumph of "technique," to be weighed against a pervasive failure of discrimination and understanding by the author. The beauty of the novel, its brilliant combining of Jane Austen's usual mastery of speech and incident with a new sense of what setting can express, serves the end of a subtler statement and development of the novelist's grasp of the fictional "life" she deals with. Though it would be hard to prove, I think we are *told* less in this novel than in her others; evaluations are less clear-cut, judgments less reliant on any moral schematism, significance more dependent on our "reading" of scenes. If we look in Fanny for the signs that so firmly place Jane Austen's other heroines we will not find them, nor are Edmund, Mary, and Henry so distinctly given moral location. But this blurring of the outlines of comedy of manners (or fairytale) creates not confusion but a new generosity and seriousness in the presentation of "theme."

The theme presented has to do with meddling, seeking to impose one's will on creatures entitled to wills of their own, treating other lives as though one's designs for them were their chief reason for being. Stated so broadly, this is the theme of *Emma* and, if less prominently, of the other novels too; at this level of generality, indeed, it is the theme of most classic fiction and many of our difficulties with life. But in *Mansfield Park* it gets a fullness of treatment not to be equalled until the triumphs of George Eliot and James.

There is first Mrs. Norris, whose selfish meddling is the novelist's hint of deeper significance elsewhere. Miss Lascelles remarks that her favorite phrase is "between ourselves," "with its suggestions of conspiracy and wire-pulling"; to this might be added the set of variations—"I perfectly comprehend you," "I entirely agree with you," "that is exactly what I think," etc.—that at least once reveals its theme: " 'If I were you.' " Mrs. Norris, in other ways demonstrably Jane Austen's most nearly psychotic creation, yearns to merge with other existences, and she deeply resents resistence:

> [Fanny] likes to go her own way to work; she does not like to be dictated to; she takes her own independent walk whenever she can; she certainly has a little spirit of secrecy, and independence, and nonsense, about her, which I would advise her to get the better of.

Although Sir Thomas, recently guilty of the same view, thinks this unjust, Mrs. Norris has put her finger on something. Behind her softness of manner, Fanny does indeed resist, and her aunt's sense of this impels her astounding attempt virtually to *become* Fanny:

> Depend upon it, it is not you that are wanted; depend upon it it is me (looking at the butler) but you are so very eager to put yourself forward. What should Sir Thomas want you for? It is me, Baddeley, you mean; I am coming this moment. You mean me, Baddeley, I am sure; Sir Thomas wants me, not Miss Price.

For an appalling moment, her madness reveals itself not simply as a yearning for intimacy with Sir Thomas's power but as a desperate hunger for the identities of other people, even the most insignificant.

But the contagion is wider spread. Tom Bertram's peevish complaint about Mrs. Norris—"it raises my spleen more than any thing, to have the pretence of being asked, of being given a choice, and at the same time addressed in such a way as to oblige one to do the very thing"—reveals, as Fanny sees, *his* will to have his own way, as when by extravagance he cheerfully deprived Edmund of half his income or tried to bully Fanny into joining the company of *Lovers' Vows* ("Let her choose for herself as well as the rest of us," Edmund had then to urge him). Lady Bertram is in her own vegetable way quite as selfish as her sister and daughters; Sir Thomas sadly comes to see that he had spoiled his family not only by indulgence but by repressing their moral freedom; even Edmund attempts to urge Fanny into Henry's arms. Robbing people of their choice lies at the heart of virtually every significant incident in the novel.

Something disturbingly more that a lack of sincerity vitiates the charm of the Crawfords. We notice that Henry is attracted to Fanny as to a puzzle:

> I do not quite know what to make of Miss Fanny. I do not
> understand her. I could not tell what she would be at yesterday.
> . . . I must try to get the better of this. Her looks say, "I will
> not like you, I am determined not to like you," and I say, she
> shall.

Lawrence would know what to make of this hunger for "knowing," this
will to destroy another's separateness. Henry is of course more than a
Lovelace, and his "moral taste" is sufficient to appreciate Fanny's capacity
for feeling, but the growth of his love gets consistent qualification:

> It would be something to be loved by such a girl, to excite the
> first ardours of her young, unsophisticated mind!

> [His vanity] convinced him that he should be able in time to
> make [her] feelings what he wished. . . . [His love] made her
> affection appear of greater consequence, because it was withheld,
> and determined him to have the glory, as well as the felicity, of
> forcing her to love him.

His will to dominate, to recreate the world as an image of his wishes, keeps
him from ever quite recognizing her reality as "another." Nor is this a
matter of the narrator imposing a commentary on Henry that his speech
and behavior won't support; when, for example, Mary doubts that Fanny
would much appreciate their dissolute uncle, Henry can airily reply that
"he is a very good man, and has been more than a father to me. Few fathers
would have let me have my own way half so much. You must not prejudice
Fanny against him. I must have them love one another." It is not moral
imperception—his tone suggests some amusement about both his uncle and
himself—but his determination that both Fanny and the Admiral shall be
objects to manipulate that defines the irony.

Mary is a richer figure, subject to more complex attention and concern,
but she too shows a corruption by will. As in her dismissal of time and
space at Sotherton, she likes to imagine worlds more congenial than the
real one. Edmund's simple determination to be ordained seems to her a
deliberate insult, shattering her trust in a different, imaginary future: "It
was plain now that he could have no serious views, no true attachment,
by fixing himself in a situation which he must know she would never stoop
to." She suffers from not being able to strike back at Sir Thomas, the
presumed "destroyer" of her "agreeable fancies"—"not daring to relieve

herself by a single attempt at throwing ridicule on his cause." As for any child, what others do has always direct reference to herself, as when she equates Edmund's "adhering to his own notions" with "acting on them in defiance of her." This wilfulness must, to be sure, be weighed against her appreciation of Edmund himself (as well as her dream of him as a "man of independent fortune"), and against her ability to rebuke herself: "She was afraid she had used some strong—some contemptuous expressions in speaking of the clergy, and *that* should not have been. It was ill-bred—it was wrong. She wished such words unsaid with all her heart." The dashes indicate the difficult achievement of honesty, as she resists the tempting understatements of her fault. She engages more of our sympathetic interest than her brother, but Mary, rather more gravely than Emma Woodhouse, is prey to what Jane Austen's revered Dr. Johnson called "the dangerous prevalence of imagination."

Only Fanny recognizes the perils of will, in resisting Edmund's advancement of Henry as a fit object for her reforming powers:

"I would not engage in such a charge," cried Fanny in a shrinking accent—"in such an office of high responsibility!"

"As usual, believing yourself unequal to anything!—fancying every thing too much for you!"

Edmund seldom appreciates subtlety; far from "fancying," Fanny here recognizes both the difficulty and the impropriety of disturbing the existences of other people, however bad. She comes as close as she can to explaining this when Henry seeks to draw her into intimacy by soliciting her advice:

"When you give me your opinion, I always know what is right. Your judgment is my rule of right."

"Oh, no!—do not say so. We have all a better guide in ourselves, if we would attend to it, than any other person can be."

The reader who thinks Conscience a quaint concept is (as he deserves to be) in trouble here. Fanny's inner guide is her only defense against will, her own or someone else's. *Mansfield Park,* a novel without miracles, has no instance of one character converting another by sitting down for a good, serious talk. Rather, those who have a conscience, like Edmund and Sir Thomas, work out their salvations in the quiet privacy of their own thoughts, while those who have none, like Henry and Mrs. Norris, or who cannot find the privacy to listen to theirs, like Mary and Maria, find no refuge from the desolations that the will insists on.

Indeed, had Jane Austen wanted to continue the pattern of titles begun with *Sense and Sensibility* and *Pride and Prejudice,* she might have called *Mansfield Park* (inelegantly enough) *Conscience and Consciousness.* Opposed to conscience, the inner guide, is "consciousness" in a common eighteenth-century sense: "Having one's thoughts and attention unduly centred in one's own personality; and hence, apt to imagine that one is the object of observation by others; Self-conscious" [*OED*]. (C. S. Lewis, who rejects this meaning as a semantic impossibility, offers another equally relevant—having a secret which you think someone shares—and admits that being in such a state may make you be and look "self-conscious.") In *Mansfield Park,* people are constantly watching one another, gauging their effect on their listeners, searching, as in a mirror, for signs of their own existence. The Crawfords, if not the source of the infection, are at least the agents of its spread. When Mary congratulates Lady Bertram upon the peace which, for bystanders, must follow the selection of *Lovers' Vows,* she remarks: " 'I do sincerely give you joy, madam, as well as Mrs. Norris, and every body else who is in the same predicament,' glancing half fearfully, half slyly, beyond Fanny to Edmund." Such consciousness is usual in Mary's conversation: "Miss Crawford turned her eye on [Fanny], as if wanting to hear or see more, and then laughingly said, 'Oh! yes, missed as every noisy evil is missed when it is taken away. . . . But I am not fishing; don't compliment me.' " And even her letter-writing is tainted:

> To have such a fine young man cut off in the flower of his days, is most melancholy. Poor Sir Thomas will feel it dreadfully. I really am quite agitated on the subject. Fanny, Fanny, I see you smile, and look cunning, but upon my honour, I never bribed a physician in my life.

For her, being conscious is a way of achieving relationship—she shares with others the amusing pretence of her wickedness and thus assures them that it *is* a pretence—and so of assimilating people to the needs of her will. That we are made to see it partly as a pathetic effort to escape isolation in the self is a tribute to the fairness and compassion with which Jane Austen presents Mary.

Because less is at stake for him, Henry's more assured consciousness can be drawn with a lighter touch. In the fine comedy of chapter 34, his reading of Shakespeare, his renouncing of amateur theatricals, and his discussion of preaching with Edmund are all calculated for their effect on Fanny, whom he keeps looking at and interrogating:

". . . nineteen times out of twenty I am thinking how such a prayer ought to be read, and longing to have it to read myself—Did you speak?" stepping eagerly to Fanny, and addressing her in a softened voice; and upon her saying, "No," he added, "Are you sure you did not speak? I saw your lips move. I fancied that you might be going to tell me I *ought* to be more attentive, and not *allow* my thoughts to wander. Are you not going to tell me so?"

"No, indeed, you know your duty too well for me to—even supposing—"

She stopt, felt herself getting into a puzzle, and could not be prevailed on to add another word.

The strands of the theme come together. Henry's will to compel her love, however comically softened, aims at incorporating her into his performance—even to the extent of writing her lines for her—and her conscience, which again forbids her to dictate to anyone, is touchingly endangered by the whisper of imagination ("even supposing"). Henry watches Fanny, Edmund (unwittingly drawn into the mannerisms of conscious play) watches them both, and with Jane Austen we watch them all. But at the center Henry watches not Fanny but himself as her response reflects him, enjoying (with some justice) his own performance for its sheer inventive gusto. And when he has finally got her alone:

"Do I astonish you?"—said he. "Do you wonder? Is there any thing in my present intreaty that you do not understand? I will explain to you instantly all that makes me urge you in this manner, all that gives me an interest in what you look and do, and excites my present curiosity."

But of course he can't explain, fully; involved is not simply his love as he would explain it, but a deeper self-love that can respond to others only in proportion to their potential for becoming himself, in effect, by becoming his creatures.

Mansfield Park, with its clashes of will and consciousness, is in fact a world of children, most of them struggling not to grow up. Henry has, preeminently, the child's fascination with the idea of changing his identity, as his delight in acting suggests. If Edmund can make him yearn for the clerical life, William Price, for a moment, arouses his hitherto unrecognized love of seafaring and honest toil. Or lacking other stimulus, his Protean interests can be absorbed by a game of "Speculation," with an opportunity to manage other hands than his own. But play is more than a relief from boredom. The planned performance of *Lovers' Vows* is wrong, I think, because it uses the theatrical blurring of art and life in the service of calculated dalliance. Mary inquires: "What gentleman among you am I to have the pleasure of making love to?", and as usual the joke is no joke at all for those who share her consciousness. Both Mr. Trilling's idea about the moral dangers of "impersonation" and Miss Lascelles's remark that Jane Austen disapproves of "make-believe that is *not* acting" are pertinent. Mary and Henry use the play to approach closer to their objects, and those objects, Maria consciously and Edmund confusedly, understand this and accept it. They are not acting but disguising emotional reality in art; but in another sense the Crawfords are *always* acting—life and art are for them not distinct, and to draw Maria and Edmund into their impersonations, for which the play is only a more or less acceptable public vehicle, is to threaten their living identities without exposing their own in return.

That they all sense this appears in their response to Sir Thomas's surprise return, which Jane Austen describes as "consternation," "a moment of absolute horror." The terms are excessive only if measured by adult values, and these are not the ones that apply:

> after the first starts and exclamations, not a word was spoken for half a minute; each with an altered countenance was looking at some other, and almost each was feeling it a stroke the most unwelcome, most ill-timed, most appalling! . . . Every other heart [except Yates's and Rushworth's] was sinking under some degree of self-condemnation or undefined alarm, every other heart was suggesting "What will become of us? What is to be done now?" It was a terrible pause. . . . Jealousy and bitterness had been suspended; selfishness was lost in the common cause.

This is more than idle mock-heroic fun; they respond like children who have been caught at some nasty, secret indulgence, and they know it and can only unite in their guilt. The horror is quite real and, from their viewpoint, quite justified, although they soon discover that the adult view—Sir Thomas's—is more liberal than they had supposed. It is a crucial moment when Sir Thomas steps into his billiard room and finds himself on the stage of a theater, "opposed by a ranting young man, who appeared likely to knock him down backwards"; but adult equilibrium is equal to the threat, the stage comes quietly down, and art and life momentarily get sorted out.

There is little charm in these children, whose dominant emotion seems to be malice. Mary recommends Henry to Fanny by celebrating "the glory of fixing one who has been shot at by so many; of having it in one's power to pay off the debts of one's sex! Oh, I am sure it is not in woman's nature to refuse such a triumph." One suspects she has been reading Etherege, but the life she observed at the Admiral's was fairly Etheregean, and her relish in the idea of "paying off" someone recalls her thwarted wish to hit back at Sir Thomas. Even cruder malice impels Tom's and Maria's "glee" at Edmund's descent from "that moral elevation" they have always resented, when he agrees to act in the play, and in Maria's struggle with Julia for Henry's attentions:

> Maria felt her triumph, and pursued her purpose careless of Julia; and Julia could never see Maria distinguished by Henry Crawford, without trusting that it would create jealousy, and bring a public disturbance at last.
>
> Fanny saw and pitied much of this in Julia; but there was no outward fellowship between them. Julia made no communication, and Fanny took no liberties. They were two solitary sufferers, or connected only by Fanny's consciousness.

In this nursery-world of aggression and spite, only Fanny has full consciousness in the better sense, sympathetic understanding of what others feel. She too is a child—witness her timid withdrawals to her "nest of comforts" in the East room—but only in her (and to some extent, Edmund) is childhood given its happier associations of innocence and tender affection.

But while Fanny measures the profound moral disturbances in her companions, she is scarcely the monument of feckless virtue she has been taken to be. Though she lacks irony, she has a streak of disconcerting common sense that has almost equal force, as in her mild remark that "let him have all the perfections in the world, I think it ought not to be set down as certain, that a man must be acceptable to every woman he may happen to like himself." Nor is she sentimentally exempted from Jane Austen's ironic scrutiny, as her fondness for quoting Scott warns us. We hear of her "feeling neglected, and . . . struggling against discontent and envy"; we see her hardly able to suppress laughter when Tom's rude remark about Dr. Grant is almost overheard; we see her in the grip of abysmal self-pity for having excluded herself from the play, where the proper response is not simple commiseration but a reflection that if she *will* insist on being good, she had better learn to value virtue properly, by experiencing its cost.

For all her affectionate concern for Fanny, Jane Austen keeps her distance even in the later episodes, when Fanny begins to grow up. Most notably, we see her human limitations in her reactions to Edmund and Mary. "It was barbarous to be happy when Edmund was suffering. Yet some happiness must and would arise, from the very conviction, that he did suffer." Edmund's defense of Mary provokes something close to venom:

'Tis nonsense all. She loves nobody but herself and her brother. Her friends leading her astray for years! She is quite as likely to have led *them* astray. They have all, perhaps, been corrupting one another.

She can quite unfairly attribute Mary's renewed interest in Edmund to his monetary prospects when Tom seems near death—Mary's motive is surely not simple greed but the feeling that being a clergyman's wife would be pleasant if one could cut a figure of style. After Edmund gives Mary up, Fanny tells him of her interest in Tom's dying—perfect delicacy might after all have spared Mary *this;* and Fanny's reaction to Edmund's misery is decidedly mixed:

She knew [he was suffering], and was sorry; but it was with a sorrow so founded on satisfaction, so tending to ease, and so much in harmony with every dearest sensation, that there are few who might not have been glad to exchange their greatest gaiety for it.

This wry assessment, taken with the other revelations of her imperfection, warns us not to love her too uncritically; she may be "my Fanny" to Jane Austen, but the tone of indulgent affection confesses that there may be something in her to forgive. Far from being unreasonably "protected" by the novelist, Fanny is her most vulnerable heroine, and so her most human one.

Fanny's moral views win out, but not through any betrayal of the "life" the novel has rendered. The presentation of Henry and Mary consistently reveals the psychic weakness at the heart of their apparent vitality and strength, and virtually every incident underlines their disastrous effect on people whose weakness is less talented and skilful. Limited as it is, Fanny's morality has after all a good deal to recommend it (as Mr. Trilling makes eloquently clear); to condemn *Mansfield Park* because in it "the deadly sins are passion and infidelity" is to invoke a sophistication that, with suitable subtlety in defining "passion," would have puzzled or dismayed George Eliot, James, Tolstoy, or Lawrence. But if we are chastened by Fanny's simple virtue, we are by no means invited to embrace it as some triumphant moral imperative. Jane Austen's narrative detachment in the last chapter marks not loss of interest or embarrassment about Mary and Henry, but an understanding that the union of Fanny and Edmund fall somewhat short of solving the universe. Each, for the other, represents an accepted *limit* of achievement. Fanny is what Edmund's ironically conceived sobriety of virtue has deserved, and no more.

Edmund in fact seems the most convincing of Jane Austen's heroes— convincing because he is "placed" by the reservations we are consistently made to feel about him. Both his reality and his limitations are finely secured by his account to Fanny of his final interview with Mary.

> She was astonished, exceedingly astonished—more that aston-
> ished. I saw her countenance change. She turned extremely red.
> I imagined I saw a mixture of many feelings—a great, though
> short struggle—half a wish of yielding to truths, half a sense of
> shame—but habit, habit carried it. She would have laughed if
> she could. It was a sort of laugh, as she answered, "A pretty
> good lecture upon my word. Was it part of your last sermon?
> At this rate you will soon reform every body at Mansfield and
> Thornton Lacey. . . . " She tried to speak carelessly, but she
> was not so careless as she wanted to appear. . . .
>
> I had gone a few steps, Fanny, when I heard the door open
> behind me. "Mr. Bertram," said she, with a smile—but it was
> a smile ill-suited to the conversation that had passed, a saucy
> playful smile, seeming to invite, in order to subdue me; at least,
> it appeared so to me. I resisted; it was the impulse of the moment
> to resist, and still walked on. I have since—sometimes—for a
> moment—regretted that I did not go back; but I know I was
> right; and such has been the end of our acquaintance!

There is much here to respect. Edmund tries to report honestly and fairly, to sort out truth from personal bias, and his hesitations prove his own mixed feelings. But it is *his* report, and we may assume that Jane Austen sees further. Mary's "sort of laugh" is the final victory of consciousness over both conscience and any genuine feeling; we regret it, not simply because it must banish Mary from the Mansfield world, but, more deeply, because she almost understood the issue. Her last smile even Edmund saw as possibly ambiguous, and we may find it movingly so. Is it saucy and impenitent, or is it the nearest she can come to a gesture of apology and regret? Is it, even, the neurotic's desperate plea to be understood and for-given despite all his resistances? But if we ponder what might have been, for Edmund the door must close forever; and we needn't scorn his inability to bear very much reality until we know we can ourselves. Mary's complex troubled consciousness can have no place in the settled society of Mansfield but this is a criticism of that society as well as of Mary. We may trust Jane Austen to know that the price of peace is considerable simplification.

The novelist's parting with Henry is less successful. He is called "cold-blooded" in his vanity which accords oddly with the Henry we have been made to *see* almost exuberantly enjoying his gifts; and Jane Austen seems unduly insistent about what he has missed:

> Could he have been satisfied with the conquest of one amiable woman's affections, could he have found sufficient exultation in overcoming the reluctance, in working himself into the esteem and tenderness of Fanny Price, there would have been every probability of success and felicity for him. . . . Would he have deserved more, there can be no doubt that more would have been obtained. . . . Would he have persevered, and uprightly, Fanny must have been his reward—and a reward very voluntarily bestowed—within a reasonable period from Edmund's marrying Mary.

The novel totters on the brink of a miracle. Those nervous modifiers ("deserved more," "and uprightly") leave unsolved a problem about the Henry we know. *Could* he deserve more and yet remain Henry Crawford as the novel has defined him? His attraction to Fanny stems from her resistance, from his need to prove the strength of his will by breaking hers; his seduction of (or by) Maria is no failure in him or in the novelist, but the inevitable fulfilment of his compulsive need to dominate and his passion to change identities. Children do grow up, and (less commonly) people do change their ways, but surely more than a Fanny Price is required to change a Henry Crawford so radically. For all Jane Austen's shrewdness about how people get married, the novel's moral design quivers for a moment.

But the miracle of Henry's redemption remains subjunctive, and I see no other flaw in *Mansfield Park*. The final withdrawal of the novelist from her created world, if it smacks a little of Fielding's excessively "healthy" scorn for those who *believe* in fiction, provides a necessary perspective on the Mansfield society. Edmund and Fanny receive an affectionate but knowing farewell, in an idiom that mocks Edmund's own fussy speech:

> Even in the midst of his late infatuation, he had acknowledged Fanny's mental superiority. What must be his sense of it now,

therefore? She was of course only too good for him; but as nobody minds having what is too good for them, he was very steadily earnest in the pursuit of the blessing, and it was not possible that encouragement from her should be long wanting.

Like Fanny, he will never quite know what he missed, and we must agree with the novelist that, on the whole, it is better that they don't.

This is not to say that Fanny and Edmund are simply the butts of Jane Austen's dark comedy. She does, however, include them in a larger field of irony that they never get out of, and thus the novel differs from her other mature works, where the heroes and heroines are either mostly exempt from irony (like Mr. Knightley or Anne Elliot), or win their release from it as the plot brings them to know what Jane Austen knows—or most of it—about life. Fanny and Edmund learn less, but that is the point; for once we are to consider how people who, like most people, have no super-abundance of wit and charm and wisdom are to get along in the world. They get along, quite simply, by avoiding what they cannot understand, which in *Mansfield Park* is the struggle of tormented souls like Mary and Henry to define their own reality by denying reality to other people. Jane Austen does not forbid us to hope that integrity and liveliness of spirit may coexist in people, but she knows that when they clash, as they often will, the latter usually wins; if we are compelled to choose, *Mansfield Park* reluctantly admonishes us to opt for integrity. *Pride and Prejudice* and *Emma* show amply Jane Austen's preference for the union of brilliance and conscience, but they show also that it may have to be achieved by virtually miraculous means, by those changes of heart that happen lamentably more often in novels than in life. In *Mansfield Park*, virtue is its own reward, and for once Jane Austen firmly insists that it may have to make do with itself. This meaning, if I am right in finding it, is no failure of the novelist's integrity but its triumph, and a prediction (as *Emma*, for all its radiance, is not) of what fiction was to be for the masters of the next hundred years.

The Improvement of the Estate

Alistair M. Duckworth

Throughout Jane Austen's fiction, estates function not only as the settings of action but as indexes to the character and social responsibility of their owners. Thus in *Pride and Prejudice* the aesthetic good sense that is evident in the landscape of Pemberley ("neither formal, nor falsely adorned") permits the reader (and Elizabeth) to infer the fundamental worth of Darcy's social and ethical character, while in *Emma* Donwell Abbey, with its "suitable, becoming, characteristic situation," is the appropriate expression of Knightley's firm sense of stewardship. *Persuasion* provides a negative example, the renting of Kellynch Hall pointing to Sir Walter Elliot's abandonment of his social trust. Landscape improvements, too, figure incidentally in all the novels, but it is in *Mansfield Park* that Jane Austen chooses to make them a recurring motif and, in so doing, to suggest an attitude to the process of social change that is central to all her fiction.

The motif is raised early in the novel during a conversation in the Mansfield dining parlor. Rushworth, the rich but stupid owner of Sotherton Court, has just returned from a visit to Smith's place, Compton, which has recently been improved by Humphry Repton, the controversial heir of Capability Brown in landscape gardening: "I never saw a place so altered in my life. I told Smith I did not know where I was." His own place Rushworth now considers "a prison—quite a dismal old prison," which "wants improvement . . . beyond anything." Maria Bertram, his fiancée, suggests that he too employ Repton, and the officious Mrs. Norris, learning

From *The Improvement of the Estate: A Study of Jane Austen's Novels.* © 1971 by The Johns Hopkins University Press.

that Repton charges five guineas a day, is quick to support her favorite niece and to seize the opportunity of spending someone else's money: "Well, and if they were *ten* [guineas], . . . I am sure *you* need not regard it. The expense need not be any impediment. If I were you, I should not think of the expense. . . . Sotherton Court deserves every thing that taste and money can do."

Interestingly, in view of her well-established viciousness in other respects, Mrs. Norris is (or was) something of an improver herself, having done a "vast deal in that way at the parsonage":

> "[W]e made it quite a different place from what it was when we first had it. You young ones do not remember much about it, perhaps. But if dear Sir Thomas were here, he could tell you what improvements we made; . . . If it had not been for [Mr. Norris's sad state of health], we should have carried on the garden wall, and made the plantation to shut out the churchyard, just as Dr. Grant has done."

I shall later argue that Jane Austen is using the technical vocabulary of improvements in a symbolic way; here it is sufficient to note that while Mrs. Norris says she has done a "vast deal," Henry Crawford is the true expert in this matter. Though the original condition of his own estate, Everingham, seemed "perfect" to his sister, Mrs. Grant, with "such a happy fall of ground, and such timber," Crawford has nevertheless "improved" it: "My plan was laid at Westminster—a little altered perhaps at Cambridge, and at one and twenty executed." Henceforward he becomes the acknowledged expert on improvements and is urged by Mrs. Grant and by Julia Bertram to lend his practical aid at Sotherton Court. Mary Crawford, it is true, finds "improvements *in hand* . . . the greatest of nuisances," but she has no objections to them once "complete": "had I a place of my own in the country, I should be most thankful to any Mr. Repton who would undertake it, and give me as much beauty as he could for my money."

Against this group of enthusiasts only Fanny Price and Edmund Bertram offer any opposition to improvements. Fanny, quoting Cowper, expresses her concern for the fate of the avenue at Sotherton which Rushworth plans to "improve" (he has already cut down "two or three fine old trees" which blocked the prospect). Her sentiments, while sufficiently romantic, are not to be read ironically. Unlike the subverted enthusiasm of the heroine in *Northanger Abbey*—Catherine "cared for no furniture of a more modern date than the fifteenth century"—Fanny's respectful attitude to the traditional aspects of the estate, like her later regret over the disuse of the chapel, is largely underwritten by her author. Edmund, for his part, though willing to admit the need of "modern dress" at Sotherton, argues against the employment of an improver: "had I a place to new fashion, I should not put myself into the hands of an improver. I would rather have an inferior degree of beauty, of my own choice, and acquired progressively."

Why Repton, and the figure of the improver generally, should so divide the characters in *Mansfield Park* is a question that seems, initially, easy to answer. Throughout Jane Austen's writing life Humphry Repton (1752–1818) was a figure of controversy, the butt of satire, and a man whose name must frequently have been on the lips of anyone connected with the land. As R.W. Chapman notes, she would have come across Repton's celebrated Red Books in some of the houses she visited, and she must have been aware of the "paper war" in which he upheld his principles of landscaping against the attacks of Sir Uvedale Price and Richard Payne Knight, the chief proponents in their different ways of the new picturesque. The context of the paper war, however, is only a partial explanation of Jane Austen's intentions in *Mansfield Park,* and to the degree that it suggests that her distaste for Repton was merely aesthetic, implying a preference for the more naturalistic styles of Price and Knight, it can be misleading. However "enamoured of Gilpin on the Picturesque" she may have been, Jane Austen commonly treats an enthusiasm for this style with some irony in her fiction—not everyone has Marianne Dashwood's passion for dead leaves. As the tone of Fanny's and Edmund's dissenting remarks in the Mansfield dining parlor suggests, moreover, she is less occupied with the aesthetic merits of different styles of landscape than with the negative social implications of a particular mode of "improvement." The important question, then, is why she chose to cast Repton as a negative social example.

A glance at Repton's *Sketches and Hints on Landscape Gardening* (1795) and *Observations on the Theory and Practice of Landscape Gardening* (1803) introduces something of a problem here, for these works reveal him to be not only an engaging, if occasionally sycophantic, writer but a theorist whose principles of landscaping often seem close to Jane Austen's own views. His emphasis on "utility," his insistence, in the first chapter of *Sketches,* upon a "due attention to the character and situation of the place to be improved" align him with, for example, Edward Ferrars in *Sense and Sensibility,* whose "idea of a fine country . . . unites beauty with utility" and who finds "more pleasure in a snug farm-house than a watch-tower." In his celebrated debate with Marianne, Ferrars's rational view of the countryside does not, of course, wholly invalidate Marianne's enthusiasm for the picturesque; like Marianne, Jane Austen was as sensitive to the "beauties of nature" as she was aware that "admiration of landscape scenery [had] become a mere jargon." But as in ethical matters Jane Austen gives priority to Elinor's sense over Marianne's sensibility, so in landscape she favors Edward's humanized, social settings to Marianne's romantic scenes. After a temporary enthusiasm for "rocks and mountains," Elizabeth Bennet in *Pride and Prejudice* settles for Darcy's tastefully improved estate.

Not all of Repton's principles of landscaping are close to Jane Austen's implied views, of course, nor was his practice always consistent with his theoretical principles. His theory, moreover, written in the midst of debate, often has an apologetic air, giving rise to the suspicion of rationalizations after the fact. Undoubtedly some of Repton's improvements fully merited the criticisms they received. While it may be true, therefore, as Donald Pilcher argues, that Repton was made "the scapegoat for the sins of [a] flock of fashionable 'improvers' " and that Jane Austen, in singling him out, both capitalized upon his notoriety and, somewhat unfairly, made him a representative of a much wider movement, it is also possible that she had a reasoned dislike of Repton's methods. Why this should be is perhaps suggested by the radical improvements Repton made at his own cottage in Essex. What he has "shut out" and "screened off" may have improved his view, but it has also removed him from any participation in the community. One wonders, in particular, what happened to the beggar (veteran, evidently, of many wars) after Repton's "improvement."

Repton's association with Capability Brown's methods accounted for much of his disrepute, for inevitably he became heir not only to Brown's practice but to the criticism that had long been directed at the "omnipotent magician" and at the figure of the improver generally. As early as Garrick's play *Lethe or Esop in the Shades* (1740), Brownian improvements had been subject to satire (Brown is here satirized when Lord Chalkstone takes exception to the layout of the Elysian fields as viewed from the shores of the Styx). Even earlier, in the country house poem of the seventeenth century, expensive innovations in estates had been castigated for their extravagance, selfishness, and disregard of "use." Thus, when Jane Austen used Repton as a negative figure, and Thomas Love Peacock cruelly satirized him as Marmaduke Milestone in *Headlong Hall* (1816), they took their places in a long tradition of anti-improvement literature.

Jane Austen's own treatment of improvements, I suspect, owes much to Cowper's *The Task*. In book 3 ("The Garden"), her favorite author castigates "improvement" as the "idol of the age" in a passage that continues the traditional complaints of the country house poem against the ostentation and hostility to tradition of the vain trustee. Here too is an awareness of the enormous transformation that improvements could bring about in a landscape:

> The lake in front becomes a lawn;
> Woods vanish, hills subside, and vallies rise;
> And streams, as if created for his use,
> Pursue the track of his directing wand.
>
> (ll. 774–77)

With her knowledge of Cowper alone Jane Austen would have been well prepared to point up the insidious implications of extreme landscaping, but she was also undoubtedly aware of Richard Payne Knight's vituperative poem "The Landscape" (London, 1794), in which Repton is bidden to "follow to the tomb" his "fav'rite Brown":

> Thy fav'rite Brown, whose innovating hand
> First dealt thy curses o'er this fertile land.
>
> (Book 1, ll. 287–88)

Even without Cowper and Knight, it is likely that Jane Austen's own experience would have led her to a dislike of the drastic alterations to landscape which frequently attended Brownian or Reptonian improvements. The radical nature of such improvements, even more pronounced in the work of less talented imitators, was everywhere evident at the time. Often involving not only the indiscriminate cutting down of trees and the magical creation of rivers and lakes but, on occasions, the relocation of whole villages which blocked the prospect and the redirection of roads by special acts of Parliament, such projects could hardly fail to strike her as emblems of inordinate change. If Edmund Burke in his political prose following the French Revolution could use the imagery of excessive estate improvements to illustrate the horrors of the revolution, we need not be surprised that Jane Austen should suggest in the adoption of Reptonian methods dangerous consequences for the continuity of a culture.

The example of Burke may be usefully extended here, not because he necessarily had a direct influence on Jane Austen's thought, but because his dislike of radical change, again and again expressed in terms of injuries done to an estate or house, suggests an appropriately serious context for her own treatment of improvements. Examples could be multiplied of Burke's employment of house and estate metaphors in the *Reflections*. Often, indeed, in speaking of the state, Burke is clearly using the image of the estate to control the construction of his thought:

one of the first and most leading principles on which the commonwealth and the laws are consecrated, is lest the temporary
possessors and life-renters in it, unmindful of what they have
received from their ancestors, or of what is due to their posterity,
should act as if they were the entire masters; that they should
not think it amongst their rights to . . . commit waste on the
inheritance, by destroying at their pleasure the whole original
fabric of their society; hazarding to leave to those who come
after them, a ruin instead of an habitation—and teaching these
successors as little to respect their contrivances, as they had
themselves respected the institutions of their forefathers. By this
unprincipled facility of changing the state as often, and as much,
and in as many ways as there are floating fancies or fashions,
the whole chain and continuity of the commonwealth would be
broken.

Constantly the need of a stable "ground" structure is stressed, as in his
expressed "prejudice" in favor of church establishment:

For, taking ground on that religious system, of which we are
now in possession, we continue to act on the early received, and
uniformly continued sense of mankind. That sense not only, like
a wise architect, hath built up the august fabric of states, but
like a provident proprietor, to preserve the structure from pro-
phanation and ruin . . . hath solemnly and for ever consecrated
the commonwealth, and all that officiate in it.

But it is not only in his veneration of traditional structures and dislike of
excessive alteration that Burke serves as a useful gloss for *Mansfield Park*.
His concept of "improvement," where this is necessary, is also relevant to
Jane Austen's motif.

As he was fond of stating, Burke was no enemy to change and improvement, and the unimproved existence of institutions is a condition
against which he constantly warns in the *Reflections*. "A state without the
means of some change is without the means of its conservation." An even
greater danger for Burke, however, lies in the overthrow or destruction of
establishments sanctioned by time and custom. Thus Burke is led, as Father
Canavan has shown, to distinguish carefully between what is necessary
improvement and what is more properly to be considered destruction.
Burke would agree with Charles James Fox in this matter that "improvements were not to be confounded with innovations; the meaning of which

was always odious, and conveyed an idea of alterations for the worse." To "improve" was to treat the deficient or corrupt parts of an established order with the character of the whole in mind; to "innovate" or "alter," on the other hand, was to destroy all that had been built up by the "collected reason of the ages." The difference is, of course, the difference between the two revolutions: the English had introduced "improvement" with their revolution, the French "innovation" and "alteration" with theirs.

It is perhaps worthwhile emphasizing the consistent antonymy of "improvement" and "innovation," or "alteration," at this period. A further passage from Burke will make the point, while a passage implicitly critical of Burke's viewpoint by William Godwin will provide the kind of exception that proves the rule. Burke writes: "A spirit of innovation is generally the result of a selfish temper and confined views. People will not look forward to posterity, who never look backward to their ancestors. Besides, the people of England well know that the idea of inheritance furnishes a sure principle of conservation; . . . without at all excluding a principle of improvement." Godwin, on the other hand (surely with this precise passage in mind), writes of "government" that it is the "perpetual enemy of change." Among other abuses, governments "prompt us to seek the public welfare, *not in alteration and improvement,* but in a timid reverence for the decisions of our ancestors . . . " (my italics). Interestingly, this passage from the third edition of *Enquiry Concerning Political Justice* (1798) is a revision of a passage in the first edition (1793), in which "innovation" is phrasally associated with "improvement." The point is clear: Godwin's association of both "innovation" and "alteration" with "improvement" is an intentional dig at Burke, as well as an indication of his diametrically opposite political ideology.

In the context of the anti-improvement literature of the time and of the political prose that frequently makes use of metaphors drawn from the practice of estate improvements, Jane Austen's motif takes on a serious meaning. In her view, radical improvements of the kind Repton made were not improvements at all but "innovations" or "alterations" of a destructive nature. No less than a political constitution, an estate, with the immaterial systems of religion, morality, and manners that it contains and upholds, will need improvement from time to time. Cultural atrophy, resulting from neglect, is to be avoided. Even more serious, however, is a too active and thoughtless response on the part of an heir. Thinking to introduce improvement, he may well destroy the "whole original fabric" of his inheritance. What has been "acquired progressively" should not be radically changed. Not to know where one is in an estate that has been "altered" is hardly the cause for pleasure that Rushworth considers it, and Mrs. Norris's "vast" improvement at the Mansfield parsonage, which made it "quite a different place from what it was when [the Norrises] first had it," strikes an insidious note in the context of Burke's prose.

Following the conversation at Mansfield there are two main episodes in the novel in which the improvements theme is taken up. The first is the visit to Sotherton, expressly made by the party from Mansfield for the purpose of assessing its "capabilities." The second occurs when Crawford proposes improvements to Thornton Lacey, the parsonage that Edmund is to occupy on ordination. The two extreme responses that are evident in these episodes help negatively to define Jane Austen's own view of what constitutes the proper improvement of a cultural inheritance.

Sotherton Court, an "ancient manorial residence of the family, with all its rights of Court-Leet and Court-Baron," is "one of the largest estates and finest places in the country." Its status as a representative estate is stressed. Edmund notes that the "house was built in Elizabeth's time, and is a large, regular, brick building—heavy, but respectable looking." Mary Crawford, while dismissing its owner, sees that "a man might represent the county with such an estate." Heavy with the air of tradition and history, Sotherton is, however, aesthetically out of date. When the party from Mansfield arrive, they find the house as Edmund described it—"ill placed . . . in one of the lowest spots of the park." With its brick construction, avenues, walls, palisades, and iron gates, it is self-evidently an estate that has largely missed the "improvements" of the great eighteenth-century gardeners. Altogether it is a "good spot for fault-finding." The interior of the house echoes the old-fashioned condition of the park, for it is "furnished in the taste of fifty years back," and though "of pictures there were abundance . . . the larger part were family portraits, no longer any thing to any body but Mrs. Rushworth." As for the chapel, built in James II's reign and "formerly in constant use both morning and evening," its function has ceased, prayers having been discontinued by the late Mr. Rushworth. Fanny, who had wished to see Sotherton in its "old state," is disappointed: "There is nothing awful here, nothing melancholy, nothing grand. Here are no aisles, no arches, no inscriptions, no banners." Like her response to the avenue earlier, Fanny's remarks are somewhat romantic (on this occasion she quotes from Scott), and Edmund gently rebukes her by describing the original modest function of the chapel. Again, however, Fanny's instinctive response is in some measure valid, for Sotherton as a functioning estate has clearly fallen into a state of desuetude. In Burkean terms "the idea of inheritance" which "furnishes a sure principle of conservation" has been lost. Here it is less important that Rushworth has come to his inheritance out of the direct line than that he has utterly no awareness of his duty as trustee. Well aware of the aesthetic deficiencies of his estate, he is ignorant of far worse ills. We gather what these are from the complacent description given by Maria Bertram, as the party from Mansfield approaches Sotherton in the barouche:

> "Now we shall have no more rough road, Miss Crawford, our difficulties are over. The rest of the way is such as it ought to be. Mr. Rushworth has made it since he succeeded to the estate. Here begins the village. Those cottages are really a disgrace. The church spire is reckoned remarkably handsome. I am glad the church is not so close to the Great House as often happens in old places. The annoyance of the bells must be terrible. There is the parsonage; a tidy looking house, and I understand the clergyman and his wife are very decent people. Those are alms-houses, built by some of the family. To the right is the steward's house; he is a very respectable man. Now we are coming to the lodge gates; but we have nearly a mile through the park still . . . it would not be an ill-looking place if it had a better approach."

Rushworth's improvements will clearly have nothing to do with his run-down cottages. His attention to the road leading to his house, like his admiration of Smith's "approach" at Compton and his later delight in wearing a "blue dress, and a pink satin cloak" for the play, reveal his character to be grounded in vanity. Nor will his marriage to Maria be the "improvement" which Mrs. Grant predicts. Maria's pride in the handsome spire shows a love of display equal to her husband's, while the pleasure she takes in discovering that the church and great house are not close is nicely ambiguous. The propinquity of house and church, common in English estates and often emphasized in Jane Austen's fiction, signifies the necessary interdependence of the clerical and landed orders. Here the physical distance between the two need have no significance, but with Maria as mistress the bells are unlikely to summon the family to regular worship, and the threat is implied that the physical gap will become a spiritual gap—a spatial correlative of a gap between, in Lord Lindsay's terms, a morality of grace and a morality of station. Rushworth and Maria will become the antitypes of the landed ideal proposed by generations of English poets:

> The Lord and Lady of this place delight
> Rather to be in act, than seeme in sight.
> [Thomas Carew, "To My Friend
> G.N. from Wrest"]

Their disregard of religion, as evident in Maria's remarks as in the present disuse of the chapel, will deny the religious dimension of landed ownership, and the displacement of their concern from the function to the appearance of Sotherton will neglect the traditional emphasis on "use" as the basis of landed existence:

> 'T is Use alone that sanctifies Expence
> And Splendour borrows all its rays from Sense.
> [Pope, "Epistle to Burlington"]

If the condition of Sotherton serves as a negative emblem of cultural atrophy, stemming from the neglect of its trustees, a second estate, Thornton Lacey, faces the even greater danger of excessive "alteration." The threat exists in Crawford's plans for its "improvement." Aware that the parsonage is to be Edmund's home on ordination, Crawford predicts that "there will be work for five summers at least before the place is live-able":

> "The farm-yard must be cleared away entirely, and planted up to shut out the blacksmith's shop. The house must be turned to front the east instead of the north. . . . And *there* must be your approach—through what is at present the garden. You must make you a new garden at what is now the back of the house. . . . The ground seems precisely formed for it. I rode fifty yards up the lane between the church and the house in order to look about me; and saw how it might all be. Nothing can be easier. The meadows beyond what *will be* the garden, as well as what now *is* . . . must be all laid together of course; . . . They belong to the living, I suppose. If not, you must purchase them. Then the stream—something must be done with the stream; but I could not quite determine what. I had two or three ideas."

What is remarkable here is how closely Crawford's proposals resemble Repton's plans for Harlestone Hall, the house most frequently considered the model of Mansfield Park. In Fragment 7 of his *Fragments on the Theory and Practice of Landscape Gardening* (1816), Repton describes his method at Harlestone:

> The House was formerly approached and entered in the south front, which was encumbered by stables and farm yards; the road came through the village, and there was a large pool in front; this pool has been changed to an apparent river, and the stables have been removed. An ample Garden has been placed

behind the house, the centre of the south front has been taken down, and a bow added with pilasters in the style of the house: the entrance is changed from south to the north side, and some new rooms to the west have been added.

Disarmed by Repton's tasteful improvements at Harlestone, . . . we may be unwilling to grant negative significance to Crawford's "Reptonian" proposals. Given Jane Austen's symbolic mode, however, Crawford's suggestions are insidious enough. His plans to "clear away," "plant up," and "shut out" features of the landscape are to be read as a rejection of a traditional shape of reality, while his wish to reorient the front of the house suggests a desire for complete cultural reorientation. Furthermore, if Repton is indeed echoed in Crawford's prose, it can be argued that Jane Austen has the latter go beyond Repton's stated practice in the *Fragments*. Whereas Repton—in the paragraph preceding the passage above—was careful to insist upon "unity of character" at Harlestone, arguing that "where great part of the original structure is to remain, the additions should doubtless partake of the existing character," Crawford is intent on completely changing the condition of Thornton Lacey; he wishes to give it a "higher character," "raise it into a *place*." (There is, of course, an additional irony in his grandiose plans for what is, after all, a parsonage.) In other respects, however, Crawford is reminiscent of Repton. His "before and after" description of the garden is the verbal equivalent of the splendid selling device Repton invented in his Red Books. There Repton masked his illustration of the scene as it would be *after* improvement with a flap depicting the *present* (and of course unfashionable) appearance of the landscape. By merely lifting up the flap a prospective customer discovered a transformation.

Edmund Bertram, however, is not tempted by Crawford's picture of a transformed Thornton. He too has "two or three ideas," and "one of them is that very little of [Crawford's] plan for Thornton Lacey will ever be put in practice." He admits that the yard should be removed in the interests of a "tolerable approach"—once again he is not averse to "modern dress"—but he will not permit the wholesale redisposition of the structure that Crawford has in mind. He would agree, one might suggest, with Burke's "prejudice" in favor of an established commonwealth—that it is "with infinite caution that any man ought to venture upon pulling down an edifice which has answered in any tolerable degree for ages the common purposes of society, or on building it up again, without having models and patterns of approved utility before his eyes."

At Sotherton, where Crawford's help was invited, his schemes may at least have helped to bring an old-fashioned landscape up to date (though, even here, there would have been misplaced priorities and emphases); but at Thornton Lacey, uninvited, his plans are not only extravagant and ostentatious, they are also supererogatory. In terms of a value system that is to be found throughout Jane Austen's fiction, Thornton is a substantial and healthy estate. The house is surrounded by yew tress and the glebe meadows are "finely sprinkled with timber." The church (unlike that at Sotherton) is "within a stone's throw" of the house; and the house itself, with its air of having been "lived in from generation to generation, through two centuries at least," is an instructive contrast to Rushworth's moribund home. One is reminded of the healthy conditions of other estates in Jane Austen's fiction and of the signs of essential soundness which she consistently provides. An abundance of timber is one such sign; the nearness of church and house another.

Trees, of course, have provided an emblem of organic growth throughout English literature. One thinks, for example, of the wych elm in *Howards End,* which, in surviving the excavations of the Wilcox men, gives some hope for social continuity. On the other hand, the cutting down of trees has suggested a radical break with the past, at least from the time of Donne's Satire II ("Where are those spred woods which cloth'd heretofore / Those bought lands?") to Ford Madox Ford's *Parade's End,* where the loss of the great tree at Groby signals the end of an order. In the light of this tradition, Fanny's objections to the cutting down of the avenue at Sotherton have deeper meaning.

In Jane Austen's fiction it is remarkable how often the presence of trees betokens value. Pemberley has its "beautiful oaks and Spanish chestnuts" [*Pride and Prejudice*], Donwell Abbey (noticeably "with all [its] old neglect of prospect") has an "abundance of timber in rows and avenues, which neither fashion nor extravagance had rooted up" [*Emma*], and there is no "such timber any where in Dorsetshire, as there is now standing in Delaford Hanger" [*Sense and Sensibility*]. It is a sign, in *Sense and Sensibility,* that the Norland estate is secure at the beginning of the novel that safeguards have been taken against "any charge on the estate, or . . . any sale of its valuable woods." Equally it is a sign of the present owner's corrupted values that, when the old owner dies, he should cut down "the old walnut trees" in order to build a greenhouse.

If trees suggest organic growth and continuity, the nearness of church and house stresses the religious content of landed life, and precisely this would be lost at Thornton if Edmund were to accede to Crawford's plans and give in to the temptation that is posed by Mary Crawford. While her brother paints his picture of an improved Thornton, Mary, hoping to transform Edmund into a man of fashion, is able imaginatively to "shut out the church" and "sink the clergyman." Like Mrs. Norris's improvements at Mansfield which, we are told, were intended to "shut out the churchyard," like Maria's pleasure in the "distance" between church and house at Sotherton, and like Mary's own response to the leaving off of prayers in the Sotherton chapel—"every generation has its improvements"—Mary's view of a future Thornton entirely excludes any sense of religious responsibility.

This, then, is why improvements of the kind the Crawfords favor are distrusted in *Mansfield Park:* they signal a radical attitude to a cultural heritage; they take no account of society as an organic structure; they effect, and indeed seem to favor, a widening of the gap between church and house, religion and the landed order.

Propriety and *Lovers' Vows*

Stuart M. Tave

If it is easier for us to mock propriety than to understand it, to see it as a foolish or pretentious or dangerously restrictive formula, it is well to know that Jane Austen was making fun of it, and seeing it also as a not so funny hypocrisy, from the time of her earliest works. As with every value, there are several false varieties and the word appears very frequently indeed in its false senses. There are the mere "rules of Propriety" that are so absurdly paralyzing on the first page of "Volume the First"; or the more threatening invocation of the word to coerce and dominate others, as it is used by the aunt in "Catharine" and by her successor, Lady Catherine de Bourgh. There is a propriety that is only the foolish fashionableness of Mrs. Elton, and the insipidity of Lady Middleton; or there is the more clever and unscrupulous exploitation of propriety by Frank Churchill and, more darkly in *Mansfield Park,* by Maria Bertram, to gain unacknowledged desires. The common element of all these versions is the silly substitution of an external form for the moral reality, or the more deliberate but still rather simple separation of the two. There is a falsification of what should be defined. But a real propriety is a true definition, in which the difficult fact and the form it ought to have are united. It is then a high sense of the shape of life. It is then an attainment of spirit and not at all easy. Marianne Dashwood may think that if there is any real impropriety she would feel it, but it is in fact only her own pleasure she is consulting; a real propriety requires a much larger vision and comprehension of many more complex parts and

From *Some Words of Jane Austen.* © 1973 by The University of Chicago. The University of Chicago Press, 1973.

an understanding adjustment of their relationships. Sir Joshua Reynolds, for example, in a difficult rhetorical situation, relative to a mixed audience and to the different kinds of advice appropriate to the several levels of his art, recognizes a problem in propriety: "It is not easy to speak with propriety to so many students of different ages and different degrees of advancement" (*Discourses*, III). In a moral situation the problems multiply as one's own integrity becomes involved, so that "an attention to propriety" follows "a habit of self-command" and "a consideration of what is your duty" (as Emma can say, if not exemplify). A moral problem may require a "delicacy" to perceive both the quality of the smallest parts that compose the whole and the manner in which they affect one another. The delicacy that is a weakness, the false delicacy that had been a subject of parody in the late eighteenth century, as it is in Jane Austen, is the accompaniment of the false sensibility that puts its willing possessor at the mercy of external or uncontrollable forces; it thereby renders him incapable of thought or action. Fanny, in her physical delicacy, has an unfortunate weakness and one the she must bear. But her delicacy of mind is a strength. A genuine delicacy is a strong form of propriety necessary for making the finest distinctions, especially in the feelings of others, and for determining the appropriate response.

When there are so many ways of losing the path, and so many forces can divert, choosing exactly the right line of conduct becomes a severe and revealing test. How difficult it can be is painfully exhibited in the major episode that leads to the climax of volume 1. The question of the propriety of the theatricals in *Mansfield Park* is frequently disturbing to readers, because it seems strange that what is, for them, such a small matter and an amusement so little threatening as play-acting at home should be taken with such solemnity and seen as such an obviously wrong thing. But the point is rather that the private theatricals at Mansfield Park are not obviously wrong. If they were they would not serve their major purpose as an episode in the novel, which is to present almost all the characters with an occasion in common, when they must make proper choices, with varying degrees of awareness, from a variety of personal circumstances, at an unusual time.

If the circumstances were ordinary and the proper conduct were evident or an authoritative voice were there to point out what should or should not be done, then Mrs. Norris would be quick to interrupt. Mrs. Norris has a quick and complete sense of propriety, she thinks. At the very beginning of the novel when she proposes that Mrs. Price's nine-year-old daughter be sent for, but Sir Thomas sees that there will be consequences for the child that must be considered, Mrs. Norris interrupts him with a reply to all his objections, stated or unstated: she perfectly comprehends him, she says, and she does justice to the "generosity and delicacy" of Sir Thomas's motives and she entirely agrees with him "as to the propriety" of doing what must be done for the child. There will be some difficulty, Sir Thomas knows, as to "the distinction proper to be made" between his daughters and their cousin, since there must not be arrogance on the one side or depression on the other, but there cannot be equality in rank, fortune, rights, and expectations. "It is a point of great delicacy and you must assist us in our endeavours to choose exactly the right line of conduct." Mrs. Norris is quite at his service, perfectly agrees that it will be most difficult, and will, with Sir Thomas, manage it easily. When he must leave his family for Antigua and is concerned for the direction of his daughters at their present interesting time of life, he has no fears because he has confidence in Mrs. Norris's watchful attention (and in Edmund's judgment). But Mrs. Norris with all her watchful attention sees nothing wrong in the theatrical amusement and when, upon his return, he expresses his surprise in her acquiescence, she is a little confounded, as nearly silenced as ever in her life, ashamed to confess "having never seen any of the impropriety which was so glaring to Sir Thomas."

The kinds of arguments offered by Edmund, who must be the chief spokesman against the scheme, show the sort of problem it presents. In a general light private theatricals are open to some objection, he says, "but as *we* are circumstanced" they would be more than injudicious. It would show great want of feeling for Sir Thomas, who is absent and in some degree of danger, and it would be imprudent with regard to Maria's situation. It is not that Sir Thomas is opposed to theatricals of any sort, any more than Edmund is (or Jane Austen). The question is one of these people in these circumstances. There is a whole series of objections, increasing in specificity and force, which Edmund raises as he sees the plans becoming more and more serious, but there is no sign that the most general, with which he begins, in the hope that they will be sufficient, are universal rules. On the contrary, at each stage his objections are qualified by someone and he must come to the next level of specificity. When he expresses his first alarm, by mock extravagant encouragement, Julia's retort is that no one loves a play better than he. He then must distinguish between real hardened acting and gentlemen and ladies struggling with the disadvantages of decorum. When this is ineffective he comes to the question of his father and Maria. Sir Thomas's degree of danger is real, not only from the normal hazards of the tropics but because of the war at sea. Tom, trying to turn that objection to a motive—the play will amuse their mother in her anxiety—sees for himself the absurdity of his attempt; no one is less anxious than their gently dozing mother. Tom then tries another, more specious line: Edmund is wrong in thinking Sir Thomas would disapprove, because Sir Thomas always encouraged their acting and reciting when they were boys. Edmund then must make the distinction between what Sir Thomas would approve in his boys when they were young and in his daughters when they are grown up, because Sir Thomas's sense of decorum, he says, is strict. Failing in that appeal Edmund then tries to limit the scale of the production, because to build a theater will be taking liberties with Sir Thomas's house and if Tom will not see that it is wrong as an innovation then he should see that it will be wrong as an expense. Step by step Edmund comes to more and more particular distinctions, relative to this family, with this father, at this time.

When the choice of play is made, that adds another level of impropriety. Fanny, who is the first to realize this, would like to see something acted, for she had never seen even half a play. So here too the objection is directed to the circumstances; she would like to see the acting but everything of higher consequence is against it. Fanny, more than anyone, understands what is happening because she knows the cross-purposes among the pro-spective actors, as Edmund does not, and therefore sees, as he does not, even more specific reasons why there is a moral problem; the proposal is bringing forth the selfishness of each actor. When the choice settles on *Lovers' Vows* she reads it eagerly but is astonished "that it could be chosen in the present instance," in a private theater, the characters of Amelia and Agatha appearing to her in their different ways "totally improper for home representation," and she can hardly suppose that her cousins can be aware of what they are engaging in.

One of the main objections Edmund has seen immediately is that the scheme would be imprudent with regard to Maria, "whose situation is a very delicate one, considering every thing, extremely delicate." Maria is engaged and hers is an engagement, moreover, that still is awaiting the return and approval of her father, who is absent at a great distance; her situation requires a more than ordinarily careful conduct. Julia understands this, but only to the end of furthering her own desires. She admits that Maria's situation may require "particular caution and delicacy," but she herself is therefore quite at liberty. Maria, to gain her desires, reverses the meaning of her engagement, using it as Henry Crawford had already used it, to raise her above restraint, with less occasion than Julia to consult either mother or father. Maria is not, here or elsewhere, an unseeing fool. After Edmund hears that the play chosen is *Lovers' Vows* and that almost every part is cast, he looks at her and asks, "But what do you do for women?" Maria blushes in spite of herself. As they argue she denies his judgment that it is exceedingly unfit for private representation, but the fact is that she has already recognized the force of his question. For us as readers the important thing is not whether *Lovers' Vows* is or is not a proper play but that Maria thinks it is not, will not let that thought balk her, and finds specious arguments. The point is emphasized by one of her arguments, directed *ad hominem* at Edmund, that she is not the only young woman who thinks the play is very fit for private representation. It is well directed because Edmund himself later gives in and becomes an actor, against his own best judgment. The size of his own later blunder, for foolish reasons similar to Maria's, is prepared for by his insistence here that it is her place to put others right and "shew them what true delicacy is," that in all points of decorum her conduct must be the law for others. "Do not act any thing improper, my dear," Lady Bertram says; "Sir Thomas would not like it." And she has said exactly the right thing, but merely as words, not knowing what she is saying, not alive enough to care, more interested in having her dinner. Nor is Mrs. Norris any more useful than her sister at the moment. Such opposition as she has made to the acting has been soon talked down and she is delighted to make the scheme an occasion of immediate petty advantage to herself and her sense of her own importance. Her attention is directed to small matters but not to the fine distinctions of propriety, to making little economies in the preparations for the play and looking about to catch a servant's boy with two bits of board, but not to the substance of the play itself: that she has never read, but she tells Edmund his objections are over-precise. Whatever small chance of success Edmund had in convincing Maria is killed by Mrs. Norris. As Mr. Rushworth is to act too, she says, there can be no harm, again missing the point. Mrs. Norris and her favorite niece are in agreement on the matter of propriety.

In Mrs. Norris's own words, her "dear Maria has such a strict sense of propriety, so much of the true delicacy which one seldom meets with now-a-days." This she had told Mrs. Rushworth just before the play-acting was suggested, during the little ball at Mansfield. What she never sees is how Maria has used and, at the very moment, is using that strict sense of propriety and the observance of common forms for purposes of particularity, for engaging Henry Crawford's attention as she dances with Mr. Rushworth. The entire history of Maria and Mr. Rushworth, which begins with the zealous promotion of Mrs. Norris, has been a very proper one. Maria has found it her "evident duty" in her twenty-first year to marry an even larger income than her father's; and so she dances with the man "at a proper number of balls"; and thus the history continues to the moment when Mrs. Rushworth removes herself from Sotherton to Bath "with true dowager propriety" and the ceremony takes place. "It was a very proper wedding." The bride was elegantly dressed, the bridesmaids were duly inferior, there were the signs of emotion as her mother stood with salts in her hand, expecting to be agitated, and her aunt tried to cry. Maria is very nearly mistress of the art of propriety as the proper show. She controls the surface. In the ride to Sotherton, spoiled for her by Julia's superior position beside Mr. Crawford, the continual prospect of their pleasure was a perpetual source of irritation "which her own sense of propriety could but just smooth over." The feelings that work uneasily beneath that smoothing over are hidden to almost everyone: to Mrs. Norris; to her father, to whom her strong passions were made known only in their sad result; to her brother Edmund, who thinks she has given proof that her feelings are not strong; to Henry Crawford, who found to his final regret that he had put himself into the power of feelings on her side more strong that he had supposed; and to herself, who did not understand their power and was destroyed by them. In the choice of the play Maria is aware to the degree of knowing the impropriety, but not to the degree of resisting it.

As the acting scheme continues it gets worse and worse, as Edmund says even as he slips into it. Fanny, pressed to take a role, and declining, begins to doubt herself and feel undecided as to what she ought to do. Once again the whole force of the episode is that it raises questions which are not simple, least so for those who are most aware of the problem of propriety. She owes much to the cousins to whom she is refusing what they warmly ask of her. She asks herself if it is not ill nature in her, selfishness, a fear of exposing herself. Is Edmund's judgment, that Sir Thomas would disapprove of the whole scheme, enough to justify her denial in spite of the other claims? Because the fears of her own retiring nature would make acting so horrible to her she is inclined to suspect the truth and purity of her own scruples. She grows bewildered. She is making an attempt "to find her way to her duty." In the midst of this, Edmund, whose judgment has been firm, whose judgment she has just been questioning only because he has been a single weight against the others, comes to her for advice. The choice of the play was bad, he says; now, to complete the business, a young man very slightly known to any of them is to be asked into their home. This is one more step in the successively important improprieties. "This is the end of all the privacy and propriety which was talked about at first." The excessive intimacy, the more than intimacy—the particularity—that will result is highly objectionable. To feel that Edmund is being rather priggish here is to lose sight of what has happened and is happening. There had been no disagreement between him and the others on the importance of the privacy to the propriety of the scheme. It was to be, Tom had insisted, nothing but a little amusement among themselves, with no audience and no publicity, just as his next assurance had been that the choice of play would be perfectly unexceptionable. Furthermore, Mary Crawford, who has been happy to take part in the acting, says openly that this admission of a stranger is unpleasant to her. In the play she will have to make love to him and, she tells Fanny, she will shorten some of his speeches and a great many of her own before they rehearse: the acting scheme will be very disagreeable now and by no means what Mary expected. This is the moment at which Edmund's judgment fails and, to prevent this next overstepping of the original plan, he decides to take the part himself. It will be, on the face of it, inconsistent, absurd, he knows, but he has heard what Miss Crawford said to Fanny and he feels for Miss Crawford. He has begun by arguing against the acting scheme in every way, and when it is past he will say "Nothing could be more improper than the whole business"; but, for all his opposition, this weakness in him has been potential from the beginning, when Mary's ready willingness to take part had, by the ingenuity of his love, turned his mind to dwell more on how obliging she was than on anything else. His present delusion appears further in his hopes that if he does enter the folly he will be in a better position to restrain it. He has come for Fanny's advice, but he does not want it. Without her approbation he is uncomfortable and knows that if she is against him he ought to distrust himself, but the strength of Mary's attraction outweighs everything.

Fanny is now the sole survivor, but the effect upon her is deeply disturbing, at first even a misery that makes her indifferent to what will happen. Though she has done nothing wrong herself, her heart and judgment are equally against the decision of the self-deceived Edmund, and his subsequent happiness in Mary's company makes her wretched. She is full of jealousy and agitation. The effect of the increasing deterioration of proprieties, then, is that no one escapes, and Fanny, having done nothing wrong, is drawn into the same whirl of unworthy emotions as the others. Excluded from the gaiety and busy employment of the others, alone, sad, insignificant, seeing Mrs. Grant promoted to consequence and honor because Mrs. Grant accepted the character she herself refused, Fanny is in some danger of envying her. What distinguishes Fanny here, and throughout, is that she is capable of thought and recovery, and in this instance reflection brings better feelings, showing her that even if she could have received the greatest respect she could never have been easy. It would have been to join a scheme which, considering only her uncle, she must condemn altogether.

She does not, even now, condemn theatricals in themselves; the others are vexed and discontented, each for his own reasons of conflict, but she derives as much innocent enjoyment from the play as any of them and it is a pleasure to her to attend the rehearsals. And her feelings about the feminine roles of the play do not arise from her own peculiarities; Mary Crawford shares them, at least to the extent of feeling the need to harden herself a little, as she says, before she can rehearse with Edmund: she hasn't really looked at the part before, did not think much of it at first, but is now examining *that* speech, and *that,* and *that.* We may recall Edmund's original point about real hardened acting and note in passing that one of the objections to ladies and gentlemen acting at Mansfield Park is not a Platonic fear of assuming a role but, rather, their amateur inability to keep their private lives from taking over their assumed roles; they don't really act. The now personal application of the part may indeed increase its attraction for Mary, but Fanny's judgment of the impropriety is corroborated. Fanny herself is again caught up in the agitation of her own emotions as she sees Mary and Edmund rehearsing and knows that she ought to stay away. The climax comes that evening when Mrs. Grant is absent and Fanny is surrounded by supplications, everybody asking that she take the part in rehearsal: this time Edmund is among the everybody. Fanny "had known it was her duty to keep away. She was properly punished." The others persevere, Edmund repeats his wish, with fond dependence on her good nature, she must yield, and the impropriety has run its full course, exempting no one. At that moment Sir Thomas returns, a dramatic and deserved little rescue for Fanny.

In the return of Sir Thomas the episode is concluded as it has begun and continued, with responses at various levels of awareness of what has been happening. Yates and Rushworth are obtuse, each in his own way, but every other heart sinks under some degree of self-condemnation or "undefined alarm," another sign that the important thing is that the participants all do acknowledge something improper has been going on. For the Crawfords, more sensible than Yates, the matter is resolved by their soon agreeing on "the propriety of their walking quietly home." But the others must stay. Lady Bertram, unusually animated by the return of her husband but, as usual, not alive to what is happening, is the one who tells Sir Thomas that they have been "all alive with acting." His reaction is not condemnation but curiosity. "Indeed! and what have you been acting?" It is not until he discovers more of the particulars of the scheme that he can judge it. Tom answers him by reducing the scale of the theatricals—something they have been doing just within the last week, a few scenes, a mere trifle. Had it been only that it would have been of less or of no importance, and Sir Thomas asks nothing more. The greater magnitude of what has in fact happened is unconsciously hinted at as Tom goes on in his attempt to distract Sir Thomas by turning the talk to shooting; he and Edmund might have killed six times as many birds as they did "but we respect your pheasants, sir, I assure you, as much as you could desire." Their serious lack of respect for his home, however, is now revealed when Sir Thomas, saying that he cannot be any longer in the house without just looking into "his own dear room," finds what changes have been made. The comic meeting of Sir Thomas and Mr. Yates, given to us through the eyes of Tom, effectively reduces Sir Thomas to a father finding himself bewildered in his own house, himself caught in the action, making part of a ridiculous exhibition in the midst of theatrical nonsense. The seriousness of what has happened grows slowly in his realization, as it grew in coming into being. The other value of showing this to us through Tom's eyes is that we see Tom understanding his father's thoughts and beginning to see more clearly than ever he had before that there might be some ground of offense. His father looks around and wonders what has been done to his home and his room. It is only much later that Tom sees other, moral, reasons of offense. Sir Thomas's gravity increases; he has been taken by surprise, "as I had not the smallest suspicion of your acting having assumed so serious a character." Tom makes a light attempt to explain the growth of the infection, as he now calls it, by saying that after Yates had brought it into the house it had spread faster because Sir Thomas had encouraged that sort of thing in them formerly. It is an attempt to shift responsibility, but it is plausible. There are many better plausible reasons that can explain. Even Edmund offers his, but now with an honest acknowledgment of his lack of judgment and deserved blame. Only Fanny, as he says, has judged rightly and been consistent, because she never ceased to think of what was due Sir Thomas.

The final judgment of what has happened is made by his father: "Sir Thomas saw all the impropriety of such a scheme among such a party, and at such a time." The impropriety is not in any one of the elements but in the qualification of each part and the composition of the whole: exactly what was being done, by whom, and when.

But having seen all that, Sir Thomas then reinforces the point for us by his own blindness. It has been disagreeable for him and he wants to forget how much he had been forgotten himself; after restoring the house to "its proper state," he says no more to his children, being more willing to believe they feel their error than to run the risk of investigation. Wiping away every outward memento, sweeping away the preparation, dismissing the workmen, and burning every copy of the play that meets his eye will, he hopes, be sufficient. In getting rid of Mr. Yates, the stranger, who he thinks has been the disturber of his home, he hopes he is rid of the worst and last object. He restores an external smoothness, calls for music, which conceals from him the want of real harmony. But we know already how much he does not see or hear and the last bit of action belongs to Mrs. Norris, who now has seen some of the impropriety but is able to foil him by her evasions and her flattery, and, ironically, by her promotion of Mr. Rushworth as his son-to-be: the theatricals end with Mrs. Norris continuing to remove an article from Sir Thomas's sight that might have distressed him, the curtain which she takes to her cottage, where she happened to be particularly in want of green baize.

Love: Surface and Subsurface

Juliet McMaster

I take the metaphor of my chapter title from Charlotte Brontë's memorable criticism of Jane Austen:

> She does her business of delineating the surface of the lives of genteel English people curiously well; there is a Chinese fidelity, a miniature delicacy in the painting: she ruffles her reader by nothing vehement, disturbs him by nothing profound: the Passions are perfectly unknown to her; she rejects even a speaking acquaintance with that stormy Sisterhood; . . . Her business is not half so much with the human heart as with the human eyes, mouth, hands and feet; what sees keenly, speaks aptly, moves flexibly, it suits her to study, but what throbs fast and full, though hidden . . . —*this* Miss Austen ignores.

It is the original and recurring objection to Jane Austen. Mark Twain (who apparently so missed violence in the novels that he thought she shouldn't have been allowed to die a natural death!), complained that her characters are automatons which can't "warm up and feel a passion." And even her admirers defended her in terms which to her detractors are damningly faint praise. George Henry Lewes announced, "First and foremost let Jane Austen be named, the greatest artist that has ever written, using the term to signify the most perfect mastery over the means to her end. There are heights and depths in human nature which Miss Austen has never scaled nor fathomed,

From *Jane Austen on Love*. English Literary Studies, no. 13. © 1978 by Juliet McMaster. The University of Victoria Press, 1978.

there are worlds of passionate existence into which she has never set foot;
. . . Her circle may be restricted, but it is complete." Elizabeth Barrett
Browning was all too ready to accept this view: the novels, she said, are
"perfect as far as they go—that's certain. Only they don't go far, I think."
"Perfect," for Mrs. as for Mr. Browning, is a term of opprobrium. It means
the reach doesn't exceed the grasp.

In the twentieth century Jane Austen certainly does not want for dis-
criminating critics who make large claims for her significance, but again
we who are her admirers have taken our stand on her appeal to the head
rather than the heart. Ian Watt quotes Horace Walpole's dictum that "this
world is a comedy to those that think, a tragedy to those that feel," and
acknowledges "Jane Austen's novels are comedies, and can have little appeal
to those who, consciously or unconsciously, believe thought inferior to
feeling." We have to a large extent conceded Charlotte Brontë's point, and
agreed that Jane Austen's business is indeed with the head and not with the
heart—we simply don't find her reaction as devastating a piece of criticism
as she evidently meant it to be: valuing as we do the activity of the mind
and the application of the intellect. We admire the unruffled surface, and
have a properly Augustan reservation about the virtues of the kind of
"vehemence" and "profundity" that Brontë misses. I myself have just been
demonstrating Jane Austen's intellectual savouring of the love convention,
and her affinities with Shakespearean comedy.

And yet . . . do we really need to concede as much as we do? In our
heart of hearts (and I use the phrase designedly) don't we know that a *full*
reading of a Jane Austen novel is a very *moving* experience, as well as an
intellectually delectable one?—that the moment of reconciliation when Mr.
Knightley *almost* kisses Emma's hand is fraught with passion, just as is the
occasion when Mr. Rochester crushes Jane Eyre to his breast in the orchard
at Thornfield, while a violent midsummer storm is brewing?

How is it done? Well, deep reservoirs may have unruffled surfaces as
well as shallow ones: if unruffled surface is what we admire, then we need
not look beyond it—and we can delight in the fidelity with which the
surface of the lives of genteel English people is delineated; but if we do
indeed value the dramatization of deep emotion, that too is there, and the
more visible, if not the more obvious, for the apparent tranquillity.

Charlotte Brontë, accused on one occasion of equivocation, vindicated
herself vigorously: "I would scorn in this and every other case to deal in
equivoque; I believe language to have been given us to make our meaning
clear, and not to wrap it in dishonest doubt." I suspect Jane Austen would
consider such a declaration somewhat crude. The naïve Catherine Morland

in *Northanger Abbey* has something similar to say of General Tilney's white lies: "Why he should say one thing so positively, and mean another all the while, was most unaccountable! How were people, at that rate, to be understood?" And Catherine's education is to involve the realization that language need not always be interpreted literally.

Of course novelists and dramatists have traditionally made capital out of a discrepancy between the profession and the reality, and many a comic scene has been built around it. Here is Becky Sharp, justifying herself to Jos Sedley when he has come to visit her in her disreputable lodgings: she has just stowed the brandy bottle, the rouge-pot, and the plate of broken meat in the bed.

> "I have had so many griefs and wrongs, Joseph Sedley, I have been made to suffer so cruelly, that I am almost made mad and sometimes. . . . I had but one child, one darling, one hope, one joy, which I held to my heart with a mother's affection . . . ; and they—they tore it from me—tore it from me;" and she put her hand to her heart with a passionate gesture of despair, burying her face for a moment on the bed.
> The brandy-bottle inside clinked up against the plate which held the cold sausage. Both were moved, no doubt, by the exhibition of so much grief.
>
> *(Vanity Fair,* chap. 65)

Becky pours out her wrongs and her griefs; the brandy bottle and the rouge-pot tell a different story. Sometimes Thackeray even provides a direct translation of the subsurface meaning. In another memorable scene between the same pair, when they nervously await the event of Waterloo in Brussels, Becky tells Jos:

> "You men can bear anything. . . . Parting or danger are nothing to you. Own now that you were going to join the army and leave us to our fate. I know you were—something tells me you were. I was so frightened, when the thought came into my head (for I do sometimes think of you when I'm alone, Mr. Joseph!), that I ran off immediately to beg and entreat you not to fly from us."
> This speech might be interpreted, "My dear sir, should an accident befall the army, and a retreat be necessary, you have a very comfortable carriage, in which I propose to take a seat."
>
> (chap. 31)

I have indulged in this little digression on Becky Sharp because she provides a convenient contrast to the usual process in Jane Austen. Becky's speech is a gush of emotion; Becky's meaning is totally a product of that energetic brain of hers, and one can almost hear the whirr and click of a calculating machine in action. Jane Austen's characters, on the other hand, conduct apparently rational conversations with each other on subjects of general interest, while simultaneously their *hearts* are deeply engaged. She is not particularly interested in the exposure of the hypocrite who uses social forms as a mask for his true motivation. Nor is Charlotte Brontë, by the way— it is notable that in the proposal scene in *Jane Eyre* Jane declares explicitly, "I am not talking to you now through the medium of custom, [or] conventionalities" (chap. 23). Jane Eyre and Lucy Snowe have to maintain a proud reticence, or burst through the barriers of convention in order to express their feelings, and when they do burst through they mean all they say; Becky Sharp and Blanche Amory are socially perfectly at ease in the display of emotion, but they mean something different. But Jane Austen's characters succeed in expressing themselves not in spite of custom and convention, but *through* them; and they mean not something different from what they say, like Thackeray's, nor all they say, like Charlotte's, but far more than what they say. So when Elinor receives Edward after their estrangement, actually believing him to be married to Lucy Steele, we can gather enough of the agonized state of her feelings by hearing merely that "she sat down again and talked of the weather" (*Sense and Sensibility*).

And here we come to her powerful use of understatement in emotional scenes. It is her frequent practice to bring a situation to a crisis, to lead you to the point where you expect some climactic exclamation of the "Great was her consternation . . . !" type, and then to report instead some apparent commonplace of behaviour or polite converse. There is a breath of a pause, a kind of hiatus between cause and effect (which I indicate typographically by a double stroke), that we learn to perceive and savour. "No sooner had Fatima discovered the gory remains of Bluebeard's previous wives, // than she made an appointment with her hairdresser"—I must invent a gross example to attune the ear and eye to Jane Austen's refined and delicate use of this device.

For instance:

Elizabeth Bennet has at last realized that Darcy is the man she loves, but just when she has come to believe that he will never approach her again. Her mother calls her to the window to see the arrival of Mr. Bingley. "Elizabeth, to satisfy her mother, went to the window—she looked,—she saw Mr. Darcy with him, and // sat down again by her sister" (*Pride and Prejudice*).

Mary Crawford, in spite of her prejudice against younger brothers, has fallen in love with Edmund Bertram. She is engaged in a game of Speculation when the gentlemen's conversation turns on the eligibility of Thornton Lacey as a gentleman's residence: "Thornton Lacey was the name of [Edmund's] impending living, as Miss Crawford well knew; and // her interest in a negociation for William Price's knave increased" (*Mansfield Park*).

Anne Elliot has steeled herself to speak to Mrs. Croft of her brother, Captain Wentworth, brave in the knowledge that Mrs. Croft knows nothing of the previous engagement:

> "Perhaps you may not have heard that he is married," added Mrs. Croft. [Anne] // could now answer as she ought.
>
> (*Persuasion*)

Again and again Jane Austen indicates a severe emotional shock by this kind of understatement. She is not *avoiding* the presentation of strong feeling; she is presenting them by indirection. It is not because her characters have no feelings that they talk of the weather and make polite responses in such moments. Words would not carry the full weight of what they feel in any case. They observe the social forms, but not at the expense of crushing themselves. For what they feel they *can* express, but they can seldom express it directly or fully: to spill out the words and feelings, regardless of decorum, is to lose the intensity, to be emotionally shallow. (That is what Jane Austen tried to suggest in *Sense and Sensibility,* when Elinor hears the man she loves is married, and Marianne goes into hysterics.) Her people speak in a succinct code, where A expresses not only A, but B and C as well.

I would like to examine, in some detail, a few passages of dialogue, and to show how polite conversation, conducted on matters of apparently general import, and within the bounds of decorum, can be informed with a subsurface level of intense personal emotion. One thing is said on the surface; but below the surface are implied the individual's ecstasies and agonies. In this way I hope to mine some of that rich and primitive ore which Charlotte Brontë misses.

I will confine myself to [*Mansfield Park*], partly for convenience (one has to stop somewhere), but also because I think that this is an aspect of Jane Austen's art which she developed and refined, and used with best effect later in her career. Lucy Steele's bitchy insinuations in *Sense and Sensibility* are relatively crude examples of a character's ability to suggest more than is stated, compared with Frank Churchill's elaborate *doubles entendres,* or with the kind of oblique communication that constantly goes on between Anne Elliot and Captain Wentworth, where, though they seldom speak to each other, each constantly understands the full import of the other's speech better than their interlocutors do. In my selection of passages I deliberately choose situations that parallel Charlotte Brontë's characteristic one, where the protagonist is forced to look on while the man she loves is courting an unworthy rival: a Blanche Ingram or a Ginevra Fanshawe, a Mary Crawford or a Louisa Musgrove. In such situations Jane Austen puts her reader on stage, as it were, since we become with the protagonist spectators who are intimately aware of unspoken implications in the exchanges we witness.

My first extract is from the famous excursion to Sotherton in *Mansfield Park*. Mary Crawford, Edmund, and Fanny, the trio who are so constantly associated, have begun to wander in the little "wilderness" of the park. Mary has just heard that Edmund is to take orders, and has had all her prejudices against younger brothers renewed. "A clergyman is nothing," she declares. Edmund defends his vocation.

> "A clergyman cannot be high in state or fashion. He must not head mobs, or set the tone in dress. But I cannot call that situation nothing, which has the charge of all that is of the first importance to mankind, individually or collectively considered, temporally and eternally—which has the guardianship of religion and morals, and consequently of the manners which result from their influence."

Mary remains unconvinced: "One does not see much of this influence and importance in society," she argues. And how can a clergyman be so influential when one "scarcely sees [him] out of his pulpit"?

Edmund tries to explain that preaching is not a clergyman's only business, and to enlarge on and explain his previous claim:

> "A fine preacher is followed and admired; but it is not in fine preaching only that a good clergyman will be useful in his parish and his neighbourhood, where the parish and neighbourhood are of a size capable of knowing his private character, and observing his general conduct. . . . And with regard to their influencing public manners, Miss Crawford must not misunderstand me, or suppose I mean to call [clergymen] the arbiters of good breeding, the regulators of refinement and courtesy, the masters of the ceremonies of life. The *manners* I speak of, might rather be called *conduct*, perhaps, the result of good principles;

the effect, in short, of those doctrines which it is their duty to teach and recommend; and it will, I believe, be every where found, that as the clergy are, or are not what they ought to be, so are the rest of the nation."

"Certainly," said Fanny with gentle earnestness.

"There," cried Miss Crawford, "you have quite convinced Miss Price already."

There is a touch of irony at Fanny's expense here. We see her as Mary sees her, as an insignificant good little thing; and she is still too much Edmund's creature, and his echo. Nevertheless, she is, with the reader, the spectator who sees more of the game than the contestants.

The dispute between Edmund and Mary is a fundamental one. It is the dispute between principle and style. For her, as for her histrionic brother, who believes he would preach splendid sermons, preaching is all there is of a clergyman, because that is all that *appears;* it is the part of his profession that can be done with distinction and applause. But Edmund refuses to divorce status from function; he deemphasizes the preaching, and insists on the practice: he is Jane Austen's version of Chaucer's poor parson. Edmund takes his stand on moral ground, Mary on aesthetic. So far they are distinguished in their general discussion on the duties and the status of clergymen.

However, the issue between them is personal and private too. In reply to Mary's gay, "There, you have quite convinced Miss Price already," Edmund urges,

"I wish I could convince Miss Crawford too."

"I do not think you ever will," said she with an arch smile; "I am just as much surprised now as I was at first that you should intend to take orders. You really are fit for something better. Come, do change your mind. It is not too late. Go into the law."

"Go into the law! with as much ease as I was told to go into this wilderness."

"Now you are going to say something about law being the worst wilderness of the two, but I forestall you; remember I have forestalled you."

Mary maintains her gay and even frivolous tone, but there is more at issue here, as all three know, than a general dispute on the merits of various professions. Edmund's underlying argument might be translated thus: "Respect the calling I have chosen," he pleads, "because I want to marry you."

Mary's underlying answer goes, "Well, I'm interested in your offer; but you must do something I think is worthy of *me*." They are neither of them fully conscious of this set of implications, but that is essentially the issue under discussion. That "Come, do change your mind. It is not too late," for all its playfulness, has its undertow of urgency.

In spite of Mary's trite witticism about law and the wilderness, Jane Austen evidently intends her readers to understand the wilderness emblematically. It was Mary who led the way into this wood, with its "serpentining" pathways, and Edmund enters it much as the Redcrosse Knight, accompanied by his Una, enters the Wandering Wood in which he encounters the female monster, Error. Related symbolism is unobtrusively developed elsewhere in the novel. Mary is the temptress, the siren, who plays the harp and sings. In another significant little scene involving the same trio, Edmund stands at the window with Fanny, who is like the figure of duty urging him to look up at the stars, while Mary goes to the piano to take part in a glee. He and Fanny agree to go out on the lawn to stargaze, but he finds himself unable to resist the music: "as it advanced, [Fanny] had the mortification of seeing him advance too, moving forward by gentle degrees towards the instrument, and when it ceased, he was close by the singers, among the most urgent in requesting to hear the glee again." This Odysseus has neglected to have himself tied to the mast. Our last glimpse of Mary is to be of her attempt to lure Edmund back to her, with "a saucy playful smile," as he says, "seeming to invite, in order to subdue me." But this time he is able to say Get thee behind me, Satan.

To return to the Sotherton scene: after Mary's sally about the wilderness, Edmund admits he can never achieve a witticism, and "a general silence succeeded." Fanny, as she so often is, has been the most acute sufferer as the witness of this veiled courtship, and presently she indicates her pain:

> "I wonder that I should be tired with only walking in this sweet wood; but the next time we come to a seat, if it is not disagreeable to you, I should be glad to sit down for a little while."
>
> "My dear Fanny," cried Edmund immediately drawing her arm within his, "how thoughtless I have been! I hope you are not very tired. Perhaps," turning to Miss Crawford, "my other companion may do me the honour of taking an arm."
>
> "Thank you, but I am not at all tired." She took it, however, as she spoke, and the gratification of having her do so, of feeling such a connection for the first time, [here one might mark another hiatus //] made him a little forgetful of Fanny. "You

scarcely touch me," said he. "You do not make me of any use. What a difference in the weight of a woman's arm from that of a man! At Oxford I have been a good deal used to have a man lean on me for the length of a street, and you are only a fly in the comparison."

Now, that doesn't sound like D. H. Lawrence. Lawrence unkindly called Jane "old maid." And she certainly doesn't expatiate on what he calls "That exquisite and immortal moment of a man's entry into the woman of his desire." But nevertheless, Edmund registers, and within the bounds of polite converse, expresses the thrill he feels at this physical contact with Mary.

There is again an emblematic quality in this threesome—Edmund between his two women, the one needing his arm, the other consenting to take it temporarily. It is a recurring triangle. Later in the novel, Fanny is the chosen witness for another such scene: this one is literally a courtship, though played as a scene in a play. During the rehearsals for *Lovers' Vows*, first Mary and then Edmund separately seek out Fanny to hear their lines in the crucial proposal scene between Amelia and Anhalt. Fanny plays her role reluctantly enough:

> To prompt them must be enough for her; and it was sometimes *more* than enough; for she could not always pay attention to the book. . . . And agitated by the increasing spirit of Edmund's manner, had once closed the page and turned away exactly as he wanted help. It was imputed to very reasonable weariness, and she was thanked and pitied; but she deserved their pity, more than she hoped they would ever surmise.

Fanny has been disliked by many because she has so much the air of a martyr; but her martyrdom is very real, for she is made to witness, and even to prompt, exchanges where the private signification is perfectly understandable and deeply painful to her.

Readers of *Mansfield Park* have often objected to what they take to be Jane Austen's summary treatment of the important matter of how Edmund, once he has lost Mary, comes to transfer his affections to Fanny:

> Scarcely had he done regretting Mary Crawford, and observing to Fanny how impossible it was that he should ever meet with such another woman, before it began to strike him whether a very different kind of woman might not do just as well—or a great deal better. . . . I purposely abstain from dates on this occasion.

But such readers have I think missed one of the major subsurface movements of the novel: Edmund's unconscious courtship of Fanny, which is concurrent with his deliberate courtship of Mary. The reader is constantly informed of how his love for Mary and his love for Fanny grow *together*. The three are always "in a cluster together," they seem "naturally to unite." The more Edmund's ardour kindles for Mary, the more fervent become his feelings for Fanny. He speaks of them as "the two dearest objects I have on earth." When he confesses his love for Mary to Fanny, he calls *her* "Dearest Fanny!" and presses "her hand to his lips, with almost as much warmth as if it had been Miss Crawford's." And when he writes to Fanny of his beloved, he tells her, "There is something soothing in the idea, that we have the same friend, and that whatever unhappy differences of opinion may exist between us, we are united in our love of you." He has indeed needed Fanny's "prompting," even in his courtship of the other woman.

Of course the psychological probability of the confidante's becoming a principal in the love affair is frequently demonstrated in literature as in life. Ritualized comic versions of the situation appear several times in Shakespeare alone (not to mention *Lovers' Vows* itself), and Fanny in her role as prompter for Edmund might well say with Viola, "A barful strife! / Whoe'er I woo, myself would be his wife!" A more serious psychological study appears in *Henry Esmond,* where the hero woos Beatrix for a decade, making a confidante of her mother, and finally marries the mother instead. And George Eliot exploited the same situation for irony and pathos in the relation of Farebrother, Mary Garth, and Fred Vincy, in *Middlemarch.*

Mary Crawford and Fanny, for Edmund, are a package deal; and at the end he simply discovers that he has mistaken the wrapping for the gift. So, in the scene at Sotherton I have been discussing, Edmund's decorous place between the two young ladies, courteously lending an arm to each, is an objective correlative for the passionate tensions of the eternal triangle.

The Promise of *Mansfield Park*

Susan Morgan

see, hear, perceive,
And cannot choose but feel.
—WORDSWORTH

Written between *Pride and Prejudice* and *Emma* and differing from both in the quietness of its heroine and the seriousness of its tone, *Mansfield Park* has developed a special reputation as the most difficult, the most complex, and therefore the most interesting of Austen's novels. What makes it difficult is finally rather simple. Fanny Price, the heroine, is so physically weak that her head aches after gathering roses, and so humble that she opens a ball with the wish that her prettier and more vivacious cousins were there to open it instead. Further, the plot is so arranged that this poor cousin of a heroine becomes the best loved daughter of the family at Mansfield Park, while all the more vivacious people end in varying degrees of disgrace. The problem, of course, is what to make of such a heroine and such a plot. Many readers, most notably Trilling in his famous essay on the book as a defense of stasis and of retreat from the modern values of openness and chance, understand *Mansfield Park* as an exception to the Austen canon. Even readers who oppose or modify Trilling's view, who see the book as modern rather than anti-modern or as flawed rather than great, still see it as unique.

There are many difficulties with seeing *Mansfield Park* as exceptional in Austen's work. Such a view assumes that there is an essential or a typical Austen heroine who is best represented by Elizabeth Bennet or Emma Woodhouse, for it is in relation to these characters that Fanny Price is

From *In the Meantime: Character and Perception in Jane Austen's Fiction.* © 1980 by The University of Chicago. The University of Chicago Press, 1980.

unusual. But this position ignores Elinor Dashwood and Anne Elliot, the
other heroines of passage, with whom Fanny has much in common. Such
a view also assumes a simplicity about the presumably typical heroines
which, for example, can lead Avrom Fleishman in a generally brilliant study
of *Mansfield Park* to claim that "Elizabeth Bennet is the fruition of a traditional type, not the first example of a new one. She is endowed with both
the wit of eighteenth-century heroines and with their animal vitality: she
is Sophia Western grown up." But this is legerdemain. Fielding's characters
do not and cannot "grow up," which is one reason why Austen's fiction
is an innovation. Moreover, if Fanny Price is the beginning of heroines
without "animal vitality," what of Elinor Dashwood? And do we really
wish to see Elizabeth's vitality as "animal" in order to distinguish her from
Fanny? What will we call Emma's?

All of Austen's heroines, both those of crisis and those of passage,
possess qualities of mind and face problems of understanding and behavior
which distinguish them in essential ways from characters in previous fiction
and connect them with many of the concerns of Romantic poetry and with
each other. What distinguishes them from each other is not whether or not
they are innovations; they all are. Rather, they differ from each other as
varying resolutions to that problem of the space between self and other
which, I have argued, is the continuing subject of Austen's work. No
appreciation of the achievement of *Mansfield Park* need require sinking the
originality of Austen's other novels. Nor need a recognition of its special
problems include seeing it as essentially different from them. Rather than
being set off from the rest, it shares with them the theme of involvement
as the basis of sound judgment.

To begin with the assumption that all of Austen's work is revolutionary
and that its focus is that difficult movement from self to outside is particularly helpful for understanding *Mansfield Park*. Such as position assumes
that we can look to understand this book in terms of its links to Austen's
other novels as much as in terms of its differences. Once the patterns of
Mansfield Park are placed within the context of patterns in the other novels
we have a way of both seeing its similarities and, in how it changes the
patterns, a way of reaching its particular meaning. Moreover, *Mansfield
Park*'s meaning can be reached and explained as a likely variation of Austen's
basic concern with perception as involvement. The familiarity of *Mansfield
Park* is that through the consciousness of its heroine it is, in Fleishman's
words, "an affirmation of a dynamic culture and a denial of the ideal of
isolation; that it stands for intense social engagement, and not for a retreat

from life; that its very subject is the misery that isolation brings, and its plea a plea for connection." The originality of *Mansfield Park* is that Austen presents its affirmation through a new sense of being in time.

Mansfield Park contains many of the patterns Austen had used in *Northanger Abbey, Sense and Sensibility,* and *Pride and Prejudice,* and would use again in *Emma* and *Persuasion.* The position of the heroine as outside, and often the observer of, relations between the hero and a rival is common in the novels. Edward Ferrars has his Lucy Steele, Mr. Darcy his Miss Bingley. Mr. Knightley will have his Harriet Smith and Captain Wentworth his Louisa Musgrove. The forms are widely varied but, if nothing else, what links the false couple is the heroine's consciousness and her distance from them. That distance is often maintained not only by a supposed rival or by the heroine's blind wishes but also by the disapproval of the hero's family. General Tilney, Mrs. Ferrars and Fanny Dashwood, Lady Catherine de Bourgh, at least temporarily, stand against the heroine's happiness. After *Mansfield Park* the dissenting relatives are from the heroine's family. Further, the heroine's sense of herself as outside may include not only watching her beloved and her rival but being taken into the rival's confidence. Lucy Steele imposes herself on Elinor Dashwood while Emma, most deservedly, must hear the confidences of Harriet Smith. Thus it is quite an archetypical Austen moment when, in *Mansfield Park,* Fanny Price is invaded in her east room and becomes the prompter of a love scene between Mary Crawford and Edmund Bertram. Nor should we be surprised that Mary imposes a friendship on Fanny which so often consists of half-confiding in, half-questioning, her about Edmund.

These repeated patterns in Austen's presentation of love relations are particularly marked in the connections and variations between *Mansfield Park* and the early novel, *Northanger Abbey.* There is an extensive similarity in the structure of relations in these two novels. The Thorpes, the false brother and sister in *Northanger Abbey,* reappear with all the transformations of intelligence and charm and money as the Crawfords in *Mansfield Park.* Isabella Thorpe, like Mary Crawford, is the older, more beautiful, more sophisticated friend of the heroine. And the heroine in both novels is a kind of anti-heroine, diffident, unsure of herself, slow in making sense of what she sees, and only sometimes pretty. For both the more sophisticated women the friendship is a means of getting to the heroine's male relative (cousin or brother). Each novel also has an older and younger brother, with the false friend drawn to the inheriting power of the elder and the heroine to the better qualities of the younger. Austen arranges these bare structures in different ways. But the base—two brother and sister pairs, one good and one false, and two brothers of which the younger is the hero—is the same.

The similarities between all the novels generally, and between *Northanger Abbey* and *Mansfield Park* particularly, make it difficult, at least on the level of plot, for me to accept that there is something unique about *Mansfield Park* in Austen's canon. The similarities do direct our reading. Thus to read Edmund and Fanny's move to Thornton Lacey and then to the parsonage at Mansfield at the end of their story as a victory of stasis and a retreat from active life seems to me mistaken on many grounds, but at the very least because one could not give the same interpretation to Catherine and Henry's move to Woodston or to Elinor and Edward's move to the parsonage at Delaford. Indeed, three of Austen's six heroines retire to parsonages and one, the one least likely to be accused of retreat from active life, marries without ever leaving home at all. Certainly, plot patterns do not determine significance. Moving to a parsonage can mean almost anything. What it means for the Bertrams is a commitment to the useful responsible life of whose "influence and importance in society" Edmund could never convince Miss Crawford.

The patterns common to *Mansfield Park* and Austen's other novels, particularly *Northanger Abbey,* are not limited only to their structures of relations and their endings. There are also explicit stylistic similarities, notably between Mary Crawford and Isabella Thorpe. Austen in her first four novels is concerned about relations between sisters, either actual or symbolic, and the pairing of a witty girl with a quieter and more candid sister is a favorite of hers. Fanny Price's character does owe something to Jane Bennet's as well as Elinor Dashwood's, while Mary Crawford has clear ties with Elizabeth Bennet, Marianne Dashwood, and Charlotte Lucas. But Mary's first link is, I think, with Isabella Thorpe. When Mary's remark to Fanny that "we are born to be connected" calls up Isabella's "there are more ways than one of our being sisters," the echo is strong enough to suggest that Mary is shallow as Isabella is shallow and that her meaning in relation to the heroine is much the same.

Mary, speaking to Fanny of Henry Crawford's proposal to her, insists that "you must allow that you were not so absolutely unprepared to have the question asked as your cousin fancies. It is not possible, but that you must have had some thoughts on the subject, some surmises as to what might be." We can hear in this Isabella's rather cruder insistence to Catherine Morland about Catherine's ignorance of John Thorpe's intentions: "Modesty, and all that, is very well in its way, but really a little common honesty is sometimes quite as becoming. I have no idea of being so overstrained! It is fishing for compliments. His attentions were such as a child must have noticed." But in spite of Isabella's "must have" and in spite of Mary's "it is not possible, but that you must have," neither Fanny nor Catherine had been prepared for those brothers' intentions. That these two sisters would think otherwise has to do with a similar way of understanding human relations. For both it is inconceivable not to be, in Mary's telling phrase, "as conscious as heart could desire." It will turn out that Fanny Price, and even Catherine Morland, are conscious to degrees beyond what the hearts of the Thorpes and Crawfords could desire, so much so that they realize what is wrong about the proposals each receives.

The Thorpes and the Crawfords are fortune hunters. The Thorpes, Austen's earlier and simpler version, wanted money. The Crawfords are already "young people of fortune." They have, as Austen so beautifully put it about Henry, the "moral taste" to seek a higher prize: the intrinsic value of good principles. But if their object is more worthy, of their acquisitiveness there can be no doubt. Part of the fascination of this pair is that superiority of taste which directs them to a higher object. With Edmund, and even more with Fanny, it is the Crawfords who most recognize and appreciate their virtues. And part of the brilliance of *Mansfield Park* is its development of the attitude of acquisitiveness from the simple materialism of *Northanger Abbey* to the desire for conquest and possession of another's spirituality. When Mary, reminded of Edmund's decision to act in the play, says "His sturdy spirit to bend as it did! Oh! it was sweet beyond expression" and when Henry lists the virtues of Fanny which were necessary to "attach a man of sense" as if he were counting up a dowry, we can see no happiness for the objects of such affections. The Crawfords, like the Thorpes, are fitted by neither their charms nor the quality of their affections to be paired with the people they would attach.

However, the similarities between the two novels are only partial. John Thorpe is horribly vulgar, Isabella is a hypocrite. The Crawfords are much finer and more serious creations. While their associations with the Thorpes can orient our judgment, understanding them is another matter. Henry becomes almost good, at least begins a way of behaving which would end in his marrying Fanny. The most immediate fact about Mary which distinguishes her from Isabella as a more complex and sympathetic character is that Mary has a kind heart or, to put it in the exact language Austen chooses when describing Mary comforting Fanny after Mrs. Norris's insult, she does have "really good feelings by which she was almost purely governed." Mary cares about Fanny, in spite of the accuracy of Fanny's prediction that she does not care enough to continue to write without the impetus of Edmund's being near enough to read the letters as well. Mary's affections often need the impetus of a little self-interest to make themselves felt to her. Still, her affection for Fanny can go so far as to let her feel that the advantage in Henry's marrying Fanny would not only be on Henry's side. And, of course, Mary can feel enough to fall in love with Edmund, though he has none of the advantages of wit or of sophisticated charm or of a Mr. before his surname. Her love for Edmund is our most essential proof of Mary's being composed of elements beyond a desire for gain.

But Mary, of course, is seriously flawed. Finally, as the plot insists in spite of Edmund's sanguine wish that the faults of her prior education can be overcome, Mary is irretrievably flawed. For Austen there always comes a point when defects of character, though they be as Fanny gently suggests "the effect of education," are not to be reversed. We laugh when Aunt Norris lectures the Bertram girls that "you should always be modest; for, much as you know already, there is a great deal more for you to learn," and one of the sisters replies, "Yes, I know there is, till I am seventeen." But education really can stop. Refusing to learn destroys the chance to learn. Mary Crawford is a great creation both because she is an interesting blend of virtues and faults and because Austen has made her a mixed character in which the faults triumph.

Isabella Thorpe, though encountered in the midland counties of England, seems to us pretty simply bad. Many of Austen's mixed characters do turn out to be fairly good, which is to say that they are educated during the action of their stories. Apart from the major heroines this is true before *Mansfield Park* of Marianne Dashwood. And it is noticeably not true of that difficult friend in *Pride and Prejudice,* Charlotte Lucas. But Mary Crawford, though occasionally with "really good feelings," is allowed no reform. If her role in the action is reminiscent of Isabella Thorpe's, her intellectual ties are with Marianne Dashwood and Charlotte Lucas. Austen's creation of Mary seems a logical, or perhaps simply a plausible, outcome of the studies of wrong-headedness she had presented in the three novels before *Mansfield Park.* With Elizabeth Bennet, Austen had defined the proper uses of intelligence, that concern for others and involvement in the life surrounding one which is the basis for clarity of vision. With Mary Crawford, older and more independent than Marianne Dashwood and more handsome, clever, and rich than Charlotte Lucas, she offers her fullest portrait of the misuse of intelligence. Mary is a powerful figure in *Mansfield Park* because she represents with charm and vividness a way of seeing and judging which Austen was continually concerned to expose. The echoes of previous characters can help us to pierce the curtain of charm, and see that intelligence need not be a question of style. Mary Crawford is Austen's vision of waste.

When we first meet Mary Crawford she echoes Charlotte Lucas. Her first topic of conversation in the novel is marriage. After laughing to Mrs. Grant about Henry's reluctance to marry, Mary gladly acknowledges that she is not reluctant: she "would have every body marry if they can do it properly," if "they can do it to advantage." The ambiguous parallelism of "properly" with "to advantage" is an early hint of Mary's false values. In her next conversation she claims that "there is not one in a hundred of either sex, who is not taken in when they marry. Look where I will, I see that it *is* so; and I feel that it *must* be so, when I consider that it is, of all transactions, the one in which people expect most from others, and are least honest themselves." Mary's verbal leap, from what *is* so to what *must* be so, reveals the fallacy of her thinking. Like Charlotte before her, Mary would deny personal moral responsibility by rendering necessary and in- evitable what is actually a matter of choice. The realist, ever invoking the way things are, thereby denies any obligation to change them. Further, that invocation also justifies selfishness. For given the way of the world, one might as well look out for oneself. As for marriage, "speaking from my own observation, it is a manoeuvring business." Thus Mary defines her relation to her own actions. She is an observer, and her own maneuverings, we are to believe, are imposed upon her by the nature of the business. When immediately after this conversation Mary considers marrying Tom Bertram, she "looked about her with due consideration," decided "it might do very well," and "began accordingly to interest herself a little about the horse which he had to run."

Once again, we are with a character, who, without thinking highly of either men or matrimony, wants to marry. And one way to measure Mary's role in the novel is that her initial opinion of marriage does not change. In that early conversation with Mrs. Grant she had claimed that, especially in marriage, "every body is taken in at some period or other." In her last interview with Fanny in the east room while speaking of her friends the Frasers, Mary uses the same language to observe that "poor Janet has been sadly taken in" and concludes that "this seems as if nothing were a security for matrimonial comfort!" This late scene reminds us that, even to the end, Mary's views of marriage are as they were. Falling in love with Edmund has not changed her attitude that happiness in marriage is a matter of chance.

Mary's wit, her easy play of words, her "*Rears, and Vices,*" comes from a satisfaction that she well understands what she thinks of as the ways of the world: no foolish illusions for Mary on the subject of marriage. Her sense of herself is much the same as Charlotte Lucas's. She sees herself as a realist, clear-eyed and practical, but with the coldness of that practicality warmed by the awareness of being both beautiful and rich. Financially as well as emotionally, Mary can afford to be romantic in a way that Charlotte could not. Still, they share a blasting cynicism, a self-satisfied conviction that they speak from an observation of extensive view. Charlotte Lucas had defended her attitude on the simple grounds of social and economic necessity. A woman, twenty-seven, poor, plain, in a limited environment, has the right to marry for the sake of getting her own home. Nonetheless, Charlotte's arguments were specious. Mary, without the arguments of necessity at her disposal, simply asserts that her views are the fundamental truths of human nature. Mary cannot bring herself to decide to marry the man she loves, though he has a profession and an income and she is a woman of fortune.

Mary's cynicism, her selfishness which passes for practical realism, extends to more than the subject of matrimony. It is a general habit of mind which, under the guise of accepting things the way they are, insists on the right to selfishness and denies obligation to others. That even Tom Bertram might deserve better than to be manipulated into marriage with a woman who does not love him would seem to Mary mere foolishness, a sentimentality. She has no sense of being unkind to Edmund in requiring that he give up his desired profession if he wants to marry her. And she easily "left Fanny to her fate" with Henry, offering only the stipulation that "I will not have you plunge her deep." It is a dog-eat-dog world, in which the fittest survive. And Mary Crawford, like her brother and the Bertram sisters, considers herself particularly well fit.

One of the most striking moments in Mary's early relations with her new acquaintance at Mansfield Park is the matter of her learning to ride. It is this incident which establishes Mary's impressive physical fitness, her "being gifted by nature with strength and courage." And it is this incident which, by odious comparisons, establishes Mary's superiority to Fanny in good health, physical bravery, and love of exercise. As the old coachman so mercilessly puts it to Fanny, "It is a pleasure to see a lady with such a good heart for riding! . . . Very different from you, miss." Not only Fanny but many readers as well have felt discomfited by the comparison. Good health is always a pleasing attribute and we are sorry to have to be involved with a heroine who trembles when she is put on a horse. But Austen astutely leaves it to Maria Bertram, a most questionable voice, to sum up that line of thinking. Maria "cannot but think that good horsemanship has a great deal to do with the mind."

And Maria is right. But what does good horsemanship have to do with the mind in the particular case of Mary Crawford? This scene is in the novel not to demonstrate Mary's physical courage and Fanny's lack of it but to be, among other functions, part of the whole presentation of Mary's kind of mind. For Mary the world is a place of struggle and competition and she sees herself as somewhat better placed, somewhat better outfitted, than most others in the race. Believing herself, to reverse Mary Lascelles's phrase about Fanny Price, a creature better furnished than those around her, Mary approaches events as virtually a sport or a game in which she has the energy to triumph. Mary's good horsemanship, her natural strength and courage, are aspects of her energy for competition and conquest. Austen had used the subject of riding before *Mansfield Park*. Part of Marianne Dashwood's self-indulgence is her initial acceptance of Willoughby's offer to give her a horse. Willoughby, of course, is a fine horseman. His favorite sport is hunting, as Tom Bertram's is racing. Both require expensive mounts. Henry Crawford too has expensive mounts, which he lends to Fanny's brother. Elizabeth Bennet, for all her vitality and liveliness, is "no horse-woman," and prefers to walk. Good horsemanship turns out to be a suspect ability in Austen's work, connected not to strength of character but to the wrong sort of mind.

Mary's physical health and courage are a sign of her mental disease. The metaphor that Mrs. Grant introduced upon hearing Mary's cynical views of marriage, that "You are as bad as your brother, Mary; but we will cure you both. Mansfield shall cure you both," reappears in Mary's typically self-assured apology for riding the horse too long, "Selfishness must always be forgiven you know, because there is no hope of a cure." For the Crawfords, as the narrator says, wished to stay at Mansfield "without wanting to be cured." When Mary goes on to assure Edmund that "nothing ever fatigues me, but doing what I do not like," we recognize that Mary's good horsemanship reflects the willfulness of a mind diseased. Selfishness, however energetically expressed, is not a proof of mental health. As [Stuart M.] Tave has so thoroughly pointed out, liveliness, of body or of mind, "cannot mean anything better than the quality of the life it expresses."

Mary's energy for conquest, which is so essential to her physical courage, is also at the center of her softer feelings. Falling in love with Edmund is one of Mary's more appealing acts. But we must notice that the quality of her feeling for him can oftenest be described as a desire to possess or control him. Control is Mary's idea of successful love. When Edmund visits the Owens family, Mary visits Fanny, in hope of some "pleasant assurance of her power." This sense of love as a struggle for ascendency, as a sport and may the best player win, is most obvious in Mary's attempts to picture to Fanny the significance of Henry's proposal. Mary sees Fanny as living out of the world and therefore unable to measure her victory: "And then, Fanny, the glory of fixing one who has been shot at by so many; of having it in one's power to pay off the debts of one's sex! Oh, I am sure it is not in woman's nature to refuse such a triumph." Fanny returns to the basic metaphor for describing Mary's quality of mind as well as Henry's when she replies that "I cannot think well of a man who sports with any woman's feelings."

That sporting sense which characterizes the minds of Henry and Mary Crawford may account for their vivacity. But for all its energy it limits what they see as the possibilities of life. If, as Mary believes, marrying is a maneuvering business, she may be able to excuse herself for her maneuverings. But she probably will not marry "to advantage," presuming that advantages may be other than material gains. With her beauty and her elegant harp and her clever sayings "at the close of every air," Mary presents a very charming picture. And we can believe that she will go on playing her harp to the admiration of many listeners. But Mary plays as a kind of Circe, "to catch any man's heart."

For Mary success is public, social, and competitive. And this is as true of profession as of love. She sees the whole question of whether Edmund will give up his clerical profession in terms of conquest. When she realizes he is soon to take orders, Mary felt it "with resentment and mortification. She was very angry with him. She had thought her influence more." The profession itself she dislikes not on any religious grounds but because it does not allow one to "rise to distinction." We are reminded of Fanny Dashwood, who wanted to see her brother, Edward, distinguished as she hardly knew what. Mary's complaint that a clergyman, unlike a soldier or sailor, does not have adequate "influence and importance in society" reveals the same criteria of surfaces as the Ferrars family in *Sense and Sensibility*.

The criteria of surfaces were expressed in *Sense and Sensibility* not only by the Ferrars family but in another way by Marianne Dashwood, with her requirement that distinction be proved by a spirited reading of Cowper. But spirited readings, either Willoughby's of Cowper or Henry Crawford's of Shakespeare, do not prove sincerity of heart. What they do prove depends on the person and the situation. The Crawfords enjoy acting. But their pleasure in it at Mansfield Park has to do with the fact that putting on the play is an extension of that game of flirtation and sexual conquest both pass their time playing. The beauty of *Lovers' Vows*, as its title suggests, is that it is only a play. There are no real vows, no involvement with someone else, no commitment, nothing in the present that binds one to the future, no continuity, no life. Yet Mary recalls it as "exquisite happiness" and Henry as an "exquisite pleasure" when "We were all alive." What they understand by being alive is for Mary exercising the power that lured Edmund into taking a part in the play and for Henry the sense of challenge provided when there was "Always some little objection, some little doubt, some little anxiety to be got over." These attitudes are much the same. For the real risks, the open future, the unknown conclusions of responsible relations the Crawfords substitute the false "employment, hope, solicitude, bustle"—in short, the safety—of life as a play. And there are no surprises because everyone knows how the play ends.

In *Mansfield Park,* as in all Austen's novels, what is evil is to mistake style for substance, forms of understanding for truth, fictions for reality. Mary understands her experiences variously as a battle for conquest, a game for victory, a maneuvering for gain. These are simply expressions of a preconceived perspective which limits how she can understand what happens to her and what her relations to others can mean. Henry, speaking of his happiness in improving Everingham, makes the unforgettable remark that "I have been a devourer." His view, like Mary's acquisitive and conquering energy, is a spiritual form of the physical appetite both are so contemptuous of in Dr. Grant. The Crawfords are continually afraid that, living in the country, they will exhaust the sources of pleasure as well as the supply of turkeys to be dressed for Sunday dinners. They believe, and this is their terrible failing, that life may be dull. Within that relation between the mind and its objects which is the subject matter of Austen's fiction, the Crawfords believe that its objects may not be enough to satisfy continuously the demands of mind. It is a failing which Austen studies again and again, most thoroughly in the book she writes after *Mansfield Park, Emma.*

The tension between London and the Park which pervades the novel can be explained as more than just a preference for country values over city ways. Austen focuses on life in the country not so much to defend life in the country as to defend life itself. In the quietest place, in the most uneventful village, there are events enough to fill the human heart. That is the lesson which Emma Woodhouse will learn. For Mary Crawford country life requires "certain circumstances" such as an "elegant, moderate-sized house in the centre of family connections—continual engagements among them—commanding the first society in the neighbourhood" in order not to be "frightful." But the fright and the dullness reside not in the country but in the mind. Mary will be dull because she casts all her experience in predictably aggressive forms.

Like Charlotte Lucas and Marianne Dashwood at her worst, Mary sees by preconceptions. And the world according to Mary is an abstract place. That is why she has no sense of process: no memory, no interest in the growth of the Grant's shrubbery, no liking for the progress of improvements. Mary's preference for things complete, her lack of any sense of continuity, means that, with all her desire for excitement, nothing very exciting will ever happen to her. She lives among the forms of her mind, with opinions as fixed as Marianne Dashwood's at seventeen and expectations as low as Charlotte Lucas's at twenty-seven. Mary sees herself as a conscious and experienced observer of the world, amused and even able to be charmed by what she terms to Edmund as "the sturdy independence of your country customs." But it is that very "sturdy" quality of Edmund's spirit she is later so pleased to "bend." What Mary imagines she may have to learn about what she wants to term "country customs" is nothing more than a new set of forms for control. At the ball Sir Thomas gives for Fanny, when Mary moves about from person to person saying the appropriate things, she no doubt believes that she has now mastered those country ways.

During Mary's first conversation with Edmund after learning at Sotherton that he is to be ordained she objects to the clergy on the grounds that it is a profession of indolence rather than of effort. When Edmund protests against this "comprehensive and (may I say) common-place censure" Mary replies that "I speak what appears to me the general opinion; and where an opinion is general, it is usually correct. Though *I* have not seen much of the domestic lives of clergymen, it is seen by too many to leave any deficiency of information." The telling point about this objection is how unthinking, even stupid, it is. The particular truth is that Edmund is neither slovenly nor selfish and, therefore, whether or not clergymen are generally slovenly and selfish does not inform us of what his domestic life as a clergyman will be. But for Mary there is no particular truth. What matters is not what kind of clergyman Edmund will actually be but rather what general opinion has already established as the nature of clergymen. The category has subsumed the reality. What is believed to be true is more valid than what is true or what will be true.

We hear, in the quiet complacency of Mary's "where an opinion is general, it is usually correct," Marianne Dashwood's "at my time of life," Charlotte Lucas's "tolerably composed" reflections on her coming marriage, and even Elizabeth Bennet's "the more I see of the world." We detect an attitude which kills the future by believing that whatever can happen has already been summed up by what has happened. And we hear again that dull tone of detachment which, by invoking general categories of understanding, would absolve the self of personal responsibility for interpreting experience and would substitute the view of judgment as a matter of mastery within preexisting patterns. Mary is predictable in her opinions, mistaken in her perceptions, and selfish in her motives. For all her courage in riding a horse, Mary is not brave enough to feel and see and judge for herself.

Mary's initial way of understanding Fanny in terms of whether she is out or not out, her need for Mrs. Fraser to approve of Edmund, her definition of the clergy, her belief that Fanny can only gauge her conquest of Henry by coming to London to see how envied she is, her reaction to Henry and Maria's running off in terms of the need to divert public opinion— these are all signs of a mind dependent on forms. Recalling Mr. Darcy's useful arrangements for marrying Mr. Wickham and Lydia Bennet in *Pride and Prejudice,* no reader need join in Edmund's horror at Mary's recommending "a compliance, a compromise, an acquiescence, in the continuance of the sin, on the chance of a marriage." Edmund's responses are more intense than anyone's less in love with Mary need be. She is no villain. But the whole novel has shown that Mary, like Charlotte Lucas, does not have a proper way of thinking. Far from consulting her own understanding and her own sense of the probable, Mary, for all her brightness, remains a reflector of external views.

Mary does not allow experience its transforming power, and her opinions remain tolerably fixed. Gifted by nature, she does not develop beyond those gifts. In this she is unlike Marianne Dashwood, who does learn during her illness to think better than she had. Marianne owed, in Edmund's parting words to Mary, "the most valuable knowledge we could any of us acquire— the knowledge of ourselves and of our duty, to the lessons of affliction." This lesson, denied to Mary, was learned through specific experiences leading to a crisis of self-revelation. Marianne shares the pattern with Catherine Morland, Elizabeth Bennet, and Emma. Mary Crawford is Austen's study of what happens when a person, vital and intelligent, faces the critical tests of her life and fails to learn from them. As Tave has said about Elizabeth, "There is no choice of standing still. . . . if she does not learn from their experience more of the world and of herself, and whom she should love, if she succumbs to disappointment, she will not be the same girl in the same place one year older. She will be worse." Mary does not change. And in Mary's fate we are again reminded of Blake's Thel. To return to what she had been is not to remain the same but to fall into Ulro, the empty hell of stasis. Our final sight of Mary, still unattached, tinged with regret, and long in finding a husband "among the dashing representatives, or idle heir apparents," is a portrait of sterility.

Austen's novels are all committed to the richness of a reality outside the mind. The commitment may ultimately be religious, a recognition of God's good world. But it is a recognition which does not demand humility. We need only think once again of Elizabeth's laughter at the end of her story or Emma's claim that she always deserves the best treatment at the end of hers. What the recognition does demand is hope, allowing oneself to care about people and events and to be affected by them. Hope means openness to the risks of involvement and change. The character in *Mansfield Park* who takes that risk is Fanny Price. But, certainly, Fanny does not change in the way Marianne Dashwood (or Catherine Morland or Elizabeth Bennet) had. And part of the particular pleasure of reading *Mansfield Park* lies in abandoning those expectations which assume that change is imaged only as a sudden or climactic or singular crisis. The difficult beauty of *Mansfield Park* lies in its offer of what else change can be.

While Mary Crawford is a more sophisticated and negative version of Marianne Dashwood, Fanny's predecessor is, of course, Elinor Dashwood. Fanny's story is Austen's second exploration of what it means to be perceptive when the difficulties of perception rest not so much in particular moral flaws or individual self-deceptions which can be cured, but in the very nature of reality and the nature of character. Once we regard *Mansfield Park* as a different working out of the same problem Austen had explored in *Sense and Sensibility* with Elinor, then the difficulties of Fanny's being a less vigorous character than many of the other heroines are resolved. *Mansfield Park* is neither an attack on vitality nor a repudiation of the qualities of Elizabeth Bennet. Fanny Price is a different kind of heroine, but the point of her story is not that she is the only proper kind. We can begin to describe what kind of heroine Fanny is by looking at her connections to Elinor.

Elinor Dashwood is the first leading character in Austen's six completed novels whom we see trying to understand and act properly in a world whose problems are not traced by her author to a special blindness or character flaw. Elinor's difficulties in judgment, and the decorum by which she gives herself space and time to resolve those difficulties are both shown to be necessary because of two facts already established in *Northanger Abbey*: that people are imperfect and that life is richer than the categories with which we give it shape. The world is a place full of secrets and getting to know even the simplest character is a matter of giving oneself time. The structure of *Sense and Sensibility* is that of a younger sister who undergoes an educational crisis and an older sister whose judgments are a continuing process shielded from its incompleteness by the forms of civility. This structure, focusing on problems of action, on how faulty judgments may or may not become irretrievable as acts, and on how the incompleteness of judgment can be reflected in behavior, is not concerned with how good judgment comes to be that way. Elinor simply has it when the novel beings.

The story of Marianne Dashwood (as well as those of Catherine Morland and Elizabeth Bennet) implies that a person undergoes a rite of passage which leads to the self-awareness that is the basis of good judgment. Elinor, however, begins with strong feelings and the knowledge of how to govern them, the very knowledge which Marianne "had resolved never to be taught." Not only could we say—in the language of *Mansfield Park*—that Elinor is already cured, it is difficult to imagine that she has ever had such a crisis. Yet we cannot conclude that Elinor was simply born with good judgment, because to do so is to negate the transforming power of experience. The gifts of nature cannot account for change. Clearly, what is needed is a narrative which demonstrates that character develops, and which presents the development apart from the suddenness of revelation. That narrative is *Mansfield Park*.

Implicit in the creation of Elinor Dashwood is the creation of Fanny Price. Elinor is already grown up when her story begins, grown up in heart and mind. But, as I have discussed, she is not a finished or perfect character. She is fallible and her recognition of her own fallibility is essential to her power to change. We watch Elinor as she struggles to shape her judgment and understand and regulate her feelings. We watch those feelings and judgments being formed and reformed as her vision and opinions change. And we watch Fanny Price do the same thing. But we watch Fanny from the time that she is very young and we see, as we could only assume with Elinor, that there was no special moment of revelation which constituted a passage into self-knowledge. Given Austen's focus on how people can change, it is appropriate that she should write at least one novel in which she traces a character's progress from childhood.

Austen introduces her heroine when Fanny Price is ten years old and we are once again directed to *Mansfield Park*'s affinities with *Northanger Abbey*. Catherine Morland too is introduced at ten. But by the end of the first chapter she is seventeen and off to enjoy "the difficulties and dangers of a six weeks' residence in Bath." It is also true that most of Fanny's story takes place when she is seventeen, and is compressed into the few months before she marries. Yet juxtaposing the two novels reveals major differences. We meet Catherine Morland at ten in order to see that she is a normal, noisy, active little girl. The years before she goes off to Bath at seventeen only preface the story. The time of *Northanger Abbey*, with its comic conflation of the heroine's life before she is seventeen and its focus on that particular period of her coming out in the world, suggests a measure of time by major significant events, by crucial moments, by those phases during which a person's life is directed or shaped by her possibilities and choices in permanent ways. This is more or less the time of *Pride and Prejudice* and *Emma* as well. The pace of *Mansfield Park* is different and so too must be our expectations of what will happen to its heroine.

At the center of the differences in expectations is a different sense of time, a sense which Austen had introduced in *Sense and Sensibility,* and went on to develop in *Mansfield Park* and in *Persuasion.* One can think of time not so much in terms of its highlights as of its passing. This is the kind of time Elinor Dashwood gives herself by means of her polite lies. The critical events and decisions which the heroine faces may be tests, but simply in the sense that events and decisions are always tests. Failures of perception, limits of judgment, can be a matter of time. And they can be corrected not only by the revelations of a moment but by the revelations which come from time passing. Fanny Price has no moment like Catherine's realization at the Abbey of how foolishly she has been thinking. Certainly, Fanny's story resembles Catherine's in that the years from ten to seventeen are condensed and most of the action takes place when she is seventeen. But Fanny's difficulties cannot be attributed simply to false structures which, during this crucial period, she learns to reject. The difficulties are in her personality and in the complexity of experience.

To consider the power of time in our lives in terms of its continuous passing as well as in terms of its markers in particular moments has aesthetic implications. The beginning and ending of a story, always problematic anyway, seem more obviously arbitrary. *Mansfield Park*'s section on Fanny's life before she is seventeen, though condensed, is still long enough to be unique in Austen's fiction. We see, in a way that we did not with Catherine Morland, that the heroine's story begins when she is ten. The action of *Persuasion* is also different from the other novels. It takes place eight years after the time in which the happy endings usually occur. These two beginnings, one early and one late, suggest that *Mansfield Park* and *Persuasion* employ an idea of time as continuous rather than as conclusive. Happy endings are not final and beginnings may also be slippery. The meaning of a story does not rest so much in particular events as in the accumulation of more events than the author narrates. Fanny's character—what she began as and what she became—is no sudden affair. In Austen's novels there are characters who do not change but whose gifts of nature, unlike those of Mary Crawford, make them good. We need only think of Mrs. Jennings or Jane Bennet. There are also characters whose changes for the better can be focused in a given space of time, characters such as Catherine Morland and Marianne Dashwood, Elizabeth Bennet and Emma. But for Fanny, as for Elinor Dashwood and Anne Elliot, time is a different story.

Fanny's different story claims, in Tave's words, that "it is Fanny who has the strength of character, and that comes by another process, for character is not a gift of nature and, so far as a life has a character, life is not a gift of nature but something made, a long and responsible history of disposition, education and habit." The need to make something of one's life is the basis of Edmund's debates with Mary on the subject of a profession. Her objections to the clergy come from a false sense that what matters about a person's life is its public distinction. That view, as I have discussed, is shortsighted. For the moral consequence of understanding the character of life as something made is not only to see the relation of the past to the present—Fanny appreciates memory, and has a very good one herself—it is also to see the relation of the present to the future and through that vision to shape one's choices. Fleishman appropriately calls Fanny "the child who inherits the future." Henry Crawford and Maria Bertram are capable of running away together, of committing the irretrievable, because they choose not to see the future in their acts. They deny continuities.

The continuity of Fanny's life begins for the reader when she is introduced at Mansfield Park. But Fanny is "as unhappy as possible," because for her this moment in not when life begins. Mrs. Norris goes so far as to concede that "I do not know that her being sorry to leave her home is really against her." The reader recognizes that Fanny's homesick tears, far from showing weak character, signal those acute feelings which will hold together the disparate events, people, and places of her life and shape them into a congruent history. These feelings which are "too little understood" by her rich relations, are Fanny's gift to Mansfield Park. It is no accident that her first happy moments there come from discussing the people she has just left with her newly met cousin and, with his help, being able to communicate again with William. The people at Mansfield, with that indifference to lives outside their own circle which Austen will comment upon again in *Persuasion,* expect Fanny to adjust to her new life by forgetting her old. Their plans for her future would annihilate her past. But Fanny does not forget. Instead, through her divided heart, she connects both worlds.

Mansfield Park is about the making of a character. Fanny begins with great shortcomings, backward in every way except in the acuteness of her feelings. The Bertrams are "a remarkably fine family, the sons very well-looking, the daughters decidedly handsome, and all of them well-grown and forward of their age, which produced as striking a difference between the cousins in person, as education had given to their address." Amongst them Fanny is the youngest, smallest, palest, least educated, and shyest. Truly, as Mrs. Norris points out, Fanny is "the lowest and last." Yet, when Fanny turns away from the gooseberry tart or confesses to Edmund her lack of letter paper on which to write William, we cannot help loving her. Nor, as Austen's choice of these touching, childish details so carefully directs, can we but believe that Fanny's difficulties will eventually be as smoothly resolved as her letter is franked. Fanny's first impressions are askew. But because she is a child, and the particular child she is, we judge her kindly. By presenting Fanny as a Cinderella figure, Austen insures both her inadequacy and our sympathy.

Beginning as it does, the direction of Fanny's story cannot tend toward revealing her flaws. But neither should we read *Mansfield Park* as simply the revelation of her virtues. Certainly, the last shall be first and Cinderella is the princess who inherits a kingdom. Fanny, too, becomes "indeed the daughter" that Sir Thomas Bertram wanted, her story ending with "so much true merit and true love, and no want of fortune or friends." Fleishman has warned us that "sooner or later he who seeks to defend Fanny Price against the dyspeptic rage of her critics tends to claim for her a higher moral level than the other characters in the novel." He goes on to define the attackers as "committed to a morality of vitality and freedom" while the defenders assert "religion, duty, and restraint." Against such alternatives Fleishman offers the corrective view that Fanny is "a frail spirit fighting the battle of life with weapons inadequate to cope with the society in which she exists." This view properly reminds us, in Tave's words, that many of Fanny's qualities "are not given to us for admiration. They are defects she must bear as best she can." Fanny is on a higher moral level than the other characters. But we need not conclude that we are to admire duty and restraint as against vitality and freedom.

Fanny, of course, is a flawed character. She has many mean thoughts about Mary Crawford, can be self-deceptively humble and transfers her jealousy to concern for a horse. She is gifted by nature, but the gifts are limited. Still, we little understand the novel by telling over Fanny's faults. Emma, for example, has a great many more. Fanny, simple, is one of Austen's quieter heroines. This does not mean that we are to admire her quietness, any more than we are to admire Catherine Morland for her frankness. We are no more required to celebrate shyness and a reluctance to open a ball that we will be meant to praise Emma's energy to be first, much as we admire her self-love. The energy we are required to celebrate is not the gift of nature. It is the energy, open to us all, to struggle against selfishness, toward self-knowledge and that generosity of mind which should illuminate our view of the people around us. That energy is as present in Fanny as in Emma, perhaps the best furnished of Austen's heroines.

Austen's claim in *Northanger Abbey* that character is mixed is still crucial in *Mansfield Park*. Most of the characters have good moments as well as bad. Mary comforts Fanny, Henry attends to some business on his estate, Sir Thomas becomes a loving father, and Tom is reformed. It is Mrs. Norris who first thinks to bring Fanny to Mansfield Park. And even Lady Bertram sends Chapman to help Fanny dress. Edmund and William are consistently good, with the exception of Edmund's self-deceptions in loving Mary Crawford and resultant manipulations of Fanny. Still, Fanny is usually the best person in the story. This is not because her negative qualities are metamorphosed into good ones, like the frog / prince or Cinderella / princess. *Mansfield Park* is not a fairy tale. The weaknesses do not vanish. Fanny may never become an entertaining dinner guest. She will never become distinguished, even at Thornton Lacey or the Mansfield parsonage, for either her horsemanship or her fearlessness of mind. But the point is precisely that Fanny is not transformed through the magic of fiction or any other black art into a perfect character. The point is that even weak characters can live good and happy lives, can struggle and endure.

The proof Austen offers of Fanny's developing character, of her endurance and the energy for change that implies, is her rejection of Henry Crawford's proposal. And William, at least, though he considers Henry "the first of human characters," is "all for love" and cannot blame. Fanny rejects Henry because she loves Edmund, because she is slow to change and he has taken her by surprise. But this is not all. Fanny rejects Henry because she knows he is unprincipled. She has seen what no one else in her household has seen—or, if they have, refused to acknowledge: Henry entertaining himself by luring both Bertram sisters into love with him. She has seen that he is a flirt. This does not mean, as Edmund at the worst of his sophistry would claim, that Henry's feelings "have hitherto been too much his guides" and he just needs a little shaping principles: Henry is a flirt not because he has been subject to feelings but because he has not. He is, in fact, coldhearted, and would warm himself upon other people's feelings, on Fanny's love or William's courage or on the emotions dramatized in plays. Henry is changeable, unreliable, temporary, because he does not feel much at all. Thus almost any new feeling is strong enough to replace an old. Henry's constancy is explicitly what is at issue between him and

Fanny. Edmund and Sir Thomas argue that Henry's "is no common attachment" because he manages to be in love with Fanny for longer than a few days, even past her refusal of him. But their arguments are specious, and Henry, who has no sense of time, history, or a continuing life, proves inconstant after all.

Fanny's view of Henry, the basis of her rejection, is produced by time and circumstance. Like Elizabeth Bennet's of the Bingley sisters, Fanny sees clearly partly because she is "unassailed by any attention to herself." Not only is her heart already given, Henry doesn't bother charming her. And by the time that Henry does decide to bother, probably because, as Mary says, "she was the only girl in company for you to notice, and you must have a somebody," Fanny has been armed against him by what she saw when he wasn't bothering. When Edmund learns that Fanny is not brokenhearted about losing Henry, in a scene looking forward to Mr. Knightley's concern about Emma because of Frank Churchill's engagement, he says that "it seems to have been the merciful appointment of Providence that the heart which knew no guile, should not suffer." It is a pleasant thought about the purity of Fanny's heart, but Edmund has long been blind about the little cousin he believes he understands so well. It may be the mercy of Providence which has saved Fanny, but it was being in love with Edmund as well. And when we recall how carefully she has hidden that knowledge we know she is not without guile.

When Mary accuses Edmund of being biased toward taking orders because he is to be given "a very good living" yet would find it "absolute madness" to take orders without one, Edmund replies: "Shall I ask you how the church is to be filled, if a man is neither to take orders with a living, nor without?" The question is central to understanding Austen's presentation of character. Fanny's refusal of Henry, like Edmund's decision to take orders, need not be without guile to be admirable. As Austen says, "although there doubtless are such unconquerable young ladies of eighteen (or one should not read about them) as are never to be persuaded into love against their judgment by all that talent, manner, attention, and flattery can do, I have no inclination to believe Fanny one of them." Fanny's securities against Henry, "love of another and disesteem of him," do not lessen her achievement in resisting him. It is an achievement which Austen qualifies both in terms of those securities and in terms of having Fanny so weaken over the course of Henry's courtship that her author can claim that had Edmund married Mary and Henry persisted, he would have succeeded. For the achievements of character are usually the result of combined factors, of advantages as well as pure motives. And it is part of Fanny's value, of her openness to experience, of that humility which allows for the possibilities of change in herself and acknowledges the possibilities in others, that she could have been eventually persuaded to marry Henry. If Henry had persisted he would indeed have developed that quality of constancy for lack of which she refuses him in the first place. He would have changed. That they don't marry is not because Fanny is too much a creature of habit, too attached to old ways. It is because Henry is.

Fanny's motives in refusing Henry, like her character generally, are mixed. What this means is not that her weaknesses and self-interest are the secret truth, hidden beneath the self-deception of being a heart that knows no guile. To understand Fanny's psychology is not to reach to an underlying fixed truth. It is to accept that character is character in action. Fanny has tried to understand Henry. She has tried in ways almost as childish as Catherine Morland's when she asked Henry Tilney what his brother could be at by flirting with an engaged woman. But Fanny has done better than Catherine. She has guessed for herself. She has seen Julia's pain and Mr. Rushworth's discomfort, she has seen Henry encourage Julia and Maria while loving neither. Even Julia's wrong feelings, even Mr. Rushworth's shallow feelings, matter to Fanny. She doesn't like games. This dislike can become silly, as when she is unable to win from William at cards. But Fanny has not the heart for victories.

Fanny has seen Henry's lightheartedness, she has seen his sports and their real consequences because she has been attentive. And she has been attentive because she takes all their lives seriously, even when they are maintaining that they are only at play. It would be unjust to suspect that Fanny notices her world because she has no part in it. Rather, Fanny takes her part as seriously as she does everyone else's. And she looks around her because she acknowledges a reality beyond herself. It is a recognition that Emma, without the advantages of "too much opposition all her life," of a lowly position and a Mrs. Norris to remind her of it, will need to gain.

Henry, when he decides that the sport he will amuse himself with "on the days that I do not hunt" is to make Fanny fall in love with him, acknowledges that he doesn't understand her: "What is her character?—Is she solemn?—Is she queer?—Is she prudish?" He wants her, instead of her present gravity, to become "all animation" when he talks to her. This is the same false thinking Austen had presented in *Sense and Sensibility,* which would identify intensity of feeling with the forms of its expression. We already know, from Elinor Dashwood as well as from Fanny, that a woman may be deeply in love with a man without saving a chair for him by her and becoming all animation when he sits in it. Fanny's gravity is not a sign of unresponsiveness but of the extent of her responses. It is because she takes her world so seriously, because she looks around her and feels what she sees, that she turns away from Henry Crawford. Her gravity and silence are signs of the intensity of her response. And her softening toward him as he tries to charm her is not the result of her beginning to feel but of the process of changing feelings as she responds to changes in him. Fanny is special because of the extent of her openness to the people around her.

Fanny's openness is why she is so vulnerable to wrong feelings and bad advice. We see her excesses in the joy with which she saves the scrap of a note Edmund had begun to write about the chain for her cross and in the ease with which Mrs. Norris can drive her to the edge of tears. That Fanny feels her fears too much is often made obvious, as in the speed with which her less susceptible sister adapts to Mansfield Park. Fanny's responsiveness makes her a continual prey to the judgments of others. Sir Thomas's argument that to refuse to please everyone but herself by marrying Henry, to dare not to love him when loving him would oblige the family, is to be "wilful and perverse" and certainly ungrateful, so affects Fanny that "she did feel almost ashamed of herself, after such a picture as her uncle had drawn, for not liking Mr. Crawford." She is most easily influenced by Edmund, whose selfish arguments on the subjects of Mary and Henry are frequently enough to "shake the experience of eighteen." Fanny is of an agreeable temper. Her "habits of ready submission," though often misplaced, are aspects of that susceptibility to others which can be both her weakness and the means to perceptions unnoticed by stronger wills. For better and for worse, Fanny cannot choose but feel.

Openness to the world is a familiar virtue in Austen's heroines. *Mansfield Park* is a study of the vulnerable aspects of the quality which will reappear as the explicit subject of *Persuasion*. Fanny's persuadableness means that she does not, even as a quiet observer, understand people in neutral ways. She is involved with what she sees. Fanny does not look for diversion or demand that life be entertaining, because she continually finds it so. Mary Crawford, herself so often "all animation," is hard to entertain because she misses so much of what might entertain her. Henry himself distinguishes degrees of entertainment as he plays his double game of amusing Julia on the drive to Sotherton while flattering Maria that "I could not have hoped to entertain *you* with Irish anecdotes during a ten miles' drive." Fanny is easily entertained because taking feelings and actions seriously is entertaining to an extent that people such as the Crawfords do not experience. What the Crawfords come to see is that such seriousness reflects a quality of mind and heart which is itself more entertaining than they had suspected before. It is a vision they cannot sustain.

If the Crawfords stand for shifting hearts, for present feelings that do not last, the character in the novel who is committed to permanent devotion is not Fanny. It is Edmund Bertram. Writing to Fanny in Portsmouth of his fading hopes after visiting Mary in London, Edmund yet insists that "I cannot give her up, Fanny. She is the only woman in the world whom I could ever think of as a wife." And even when Edmund must face that Mary was not as he thought, he maintains his commitment: "Time would undoubtedly abate somewhat of his sufferings, but still it was a sort of thing which he never could get entirely the better of; and as to his ever meeting with any other woman who could—it was too impossible to be named but with indignation." But Edmund has still to learn the power of time to "do almost every thing," particularly the power of sitting under trees on summer evenings to renew a heart. Edmund will discover, to his happiness, that what was "impossible to be named" is to be met with a woman he has known all along.

The sentimental convention of one true love is a more endearing belief than Henry's flirtatiousness or Mary's commitment to many true loves as long as they are rich and distinguished, but all are structures which impose limits on our lives. Edmund too has committed himself to truths that do not change. We hear in his claim Marianne Dashwood's assertion that one can only love once in life. Edmund, like Marianne, has accepted absolute forms according to which he would deny or rearrange his actual perceptions and feelings. The climactic representative of this attitude in the English novel may be Willoughby Patterne in *The Egoist,* who would have Clara Middleton swear that she will be true to him even if he should die, because they are engaged and love is forever, love is a sacred tie. To believe that the future cannot hold more than a single person with whom one could fall in love is egoism. Edmund, assuming that he will never feel differently than he does, assumes a self unaffected by events. He assumes a life without time. But in this story *never* and *misery* are black words, and "exactly at the time when it was quite natural that it should be so" Edmund stops suffering about Mary and comes to love Fanny.

Certainty about what is and what is not possible is a common attitude among the characters at Mansfield. Mrs. Norris arranges life for everyone, and the tone of her arrangements is perfectly caught early in the novel when she announces conclusively that for cousins to marry is "morally impossible." And we cannot but have a moment's affection for Lady Bertram when, after her sister has so thoroughly explained to her that she shall not miss Fanny, she replies that "I dare say you are very right, but I am sure I shall miss her very much." Sir Thomas, a character committed to the solidity of his arrangements for life, carefully thinks things through, and he too believes he can be easy on the subject of cousins. Mary Crawford is quite certain she knows how the world works, and Edmund is sure he knows the workings of Fanny's heart. "*Mansfield Park* is a novel in which many characters are engaged in trying to establish influence over the minds and the lives of others, often in a contest of struggle for control" [Tave]. At the base of these attempts to control is the kind of mind that is confident about predicting events and their meaning.

Sense and Sensibility is a novel with many secrets. *Mansfield Park* has an analogous form of action. It is full of moments in which someone announces that something cannot be, only to discover that it is, or that something must be, only to discover that it is not. These can be brief and comic, such as Mrs. Norris's assurance to Fanny that she must walk to dinner at the Grants, followed by Sir Thomas's "My niece walk to a dinner engagement at this time of year!" as he orders the carriage for her. The major events of the plot, Henry's proposal and his subsequent running off with Mrs. Rushworth, are shockingly unpredictable. Even Sir Thomas's return home and Henry's arrival at the Grant's dinner party are presented as surprises. Yet none of the surprises is unlikely. They are all events that might or could happen. Indeed, some of the most selfish predictions, such as Tom Bertram's that Dr. Grant "would soon pop off," do come true. It is in these terms of likelihood that the narrator describes Edmund's change to loving Fanny: "With such a regard for her, indeed, as his had long been, a regard founded on the most endearing claims of innocence and helplessness, and completed by every recommendation of growing worth, what could be more natural than the change?" The marriage of these two is far from a fairy-tale ending. Certainly, "the cure of unconquerable passions, and the transfer of unchanging attachments, must vary much as to time in different people." But Edmund's heart, like Marianne Dashwood's with regard to Willoughby, does indeed transfer that unchanging attachment. The change was not what they predicted. But far from being magical or unlikely, what could be more natural than change?

The self-confidence and assured approach to their experience of so many of the people at Mansfield is contrasted throughout the story with Fanny's humility and timidity. Nonetheless, *Mansfield Park* is not an exemplum of the scripture that the meek shall inherit the earth. Many people in Austen's fiction inherit the earth, among them such disparate characters as Eleanor Tilney and the Bennet sisters. The inheritor of Mansfield Park will be Tom Bertram. Fanny's reward, it is true, is to become the beloved daughter, and her happiness is beyond description "on receiving the assurance of that affection of which she has scarcely allowed herself to entertain a hope." It is also true that we would wish her no less. But the moral of the story is not an absolute. Our distance from Fanny remains.

Fanny's frailties are not proof that she has either the spirit of an angel or the cunning of the weak, nor do they prove that she represents a retreat from modern life. There are many means to happiness, and Fanny's story is one of them. It does not exclude the possibility of Elizabeth Bennet's or any of the heroine's whose gifts of nature are different from Fanny's. Fanny's recommendations are the recommendations "of growing worth." That is her virtue, not her timidity or dizziness in the sun. In fact, the last we hear of Fanny is of her changing heart toward the parsonage. Her story is the story of progress measured slowly, but continually. She finds happiness not because she hopes for little, not because her expectations are low, but because she is open to the possibility of joy. Austen reminds us that Sir Thomas's own joy in the union formed just such a contrast with his early opinion as "time is for ever producing between the plans and decisions of mortals, for their own instruction, and their neighbours' entertainment."

Mansfield Park is Austen's study of what time can produce when it comes dropping slow. Mary Crawford, the more powerful character, should have become better than she was. But she would not risk the loss or transformation of self which change implies. Fanny Price, with those acute feelings which made the things at Mansfield Park "perfect in her eyes," had no possibility of being uninvolved with the people around her. That was her gift of nature, the gift which made her vulnerable as well. Mary too, we know, has amiable feelings, as well as the gifts of strength and cleverness. Yet Fanny's feelings become the basis of a concern for and attention to those around her, out of which develops an understanding that others lack. We can remember her, after Edmund has left her his gift of a chain for William's cross, engaged in that happy mixture of treasuring Edmund's note while reminding herself that she can only think of him as a friend. This activity, by which she "regulated her thoughts and comforted her feelings," is the process of character development that forms the subject of *Mansfield Park*.

Fanny is a creature less well furnished, because her virtues are not simply those she was born with, virtues some are born with and some are not. To believe in change must include believing in a character not particularly gifted by nature who becomes better than she was. How many of us are born with the liveliness of Elizabeth Bennet, and with her confidence in being a complex character? Fanny's story proceeds at a creepmouse pace because hers is an alternative form of growth to the sudden leap of Catherine Morland in the hall at Northanger Abbey, and it is fed by events less clear than Mr. Darcy's letter to Elizabeth or Marianne Dashwood's near fatal illness. The greatness of *Mansfield Park* lies in the very gentleness, the naturalness, of Fanny's change. Without obvious events, without natural gifts, without major revelations, Fanny still grows. It is the chance Austen offers to us all.

Structure and Social Vision

David Monaghan

If her presentation of great houses is anything to go by, Jane Austen began to lose confidence in English landed society some time between the writing of *Pride and Prejudice* and *Mansfield Park*. In their externals, Mansfield Park and Sotherton are suggestive of much the same ideals as Pemberley. The sheer bulk of the houses and the spaciousness of their parks underline the authority of the landowners; the careful cultivation of nature, whether it be the stream at Pemberley, or the avenue of trees at Sotherton, serves as a reminder of the organic principles upon which society is founded; and the conduct of daily life with its "consideration of times and seasons" reinforces values such as "elegance, propriety, regularity, harmony." However, whereas what Pemberley symbolises is made into a reality by Darcy, neither Sir Thomas Bertram nor Rushworth does more than keep up appearances.

In Sir Thomas's case it is not ignorance of proper standards, but a kind of shyness or even apathy, that often prevents him questioning what might lie beneath an orderly surface. Sir Thomas is, for example, "a truly anxious father," but "the reserve of his manner" makes it hard for him to establish intimate relationships with his children, and he tends to avoid situations that would involve him in struggling to overcome this reserve. Therefore, simply because they appear to be "in person, manner, and accomplishments every thing that could satisfy his anxiety," he refrains from questioning the quality of Maria and Julia's education. As a result he fails to uncover

From *Jane Austen: Structure and Social Vision.* © 1980 by David Monaghan. Macmillan, 1980.

their deficiencies in "self-knowledge, generosity, and humility." Similarly, when he returns from Antigua, Sir Thomas puts an end to the theatricals, and restores order to his house, but makes no attempt to investigate the cause of his children's anarchic behaviour:

> He did not enter into any remonstrance with his other children: he was more willing to believe they felt their error, than to run the risk of investigation. The reproof of an immediate conclusion of every thing, the sweep of every preparation would be sufficient.

Not even diffidence, however, can be pleaded in defence of Sir Thomas's response to his recognition that Maria is indifferent to her fiancé, Rushworth. Concern for his daughter's happiness forces Sir Thomas to question her motives, but so "very proper" an alliance with a man who is of high rank, wealthy, a close neighbour, and the right political colour, is too attractive for him to pursue the matter very far: "Sir Thomas was satisfied; too glad to be satisfied perhaps to urge the matter quite so far as his judgment might have dictated to others. It was an alliance which he could not have relinquished without pain." Whereas Sir Thomas Bertram fails to ensure that reality matches appearance, Rushworth is too foolish even to see that anything might exist beyond appearance. Strictest "etiquette" characterises the conduct of all affairs at Sotherton, but, as in his inability to see any significance in the cessation of the custom of family prayers, and in his readiness to cut down the avenue of trees, Rushworth reveals a moral idiocy about anything more substantial.

Because of the deficiencies of its leaders, landed society in *Mansfield Park* is ripe for corruption. Maria and Julia Bertram and their brother Tom as particularly vulnerable. None of them has been taught the active principles that should underlie a concern with propriety. Therefore, they consider the rather rigid style of correct behaviour upon which Sir Thomas insists as a pointless and stifling form of oppression, and are ready to accept anything that promises "air and liberty." Edmund is a much more serious person, and has an excellent theoretical knowledge of Mansfield values. His analysis of the role of the clergyman, for example, contains within it a brilliant justification of a rural society based on the unit of the small community. Nevertheless, Edmund is in scarcely less danger. Sir Thomas's poor example has left him insufficiently informed about the practical ways in which manners are connected with morals, and this, combined with the dullness of life at Mansfield Park, makes him too susceptible to the attractions of the merely charming performance.

The situation thus created, in which great value is attached to lively manners, and moral deficiencies are either excused or even welcomed, is one that the Crawfords are well equipped to exploit. Their London ethics threaten everything that Mansfield Park represents. However, they possess exactly the kind of vivacity and wit for which all the Bertram children are looking, and it soon becomes very likely that Mansfield will yield itself up to them. Jane Austen leaves little doubt as to what will be the consequences of this. Neither Crawford has much sympathy with the country-house ideal. Henry, for example, pays so little attention to his estate at Everingham that it has come under the control of a corrupt steward, and Mary dislikes nature and is scornful of religion. Their real allegiance is to the new urban world in which "every thing is to be got with money" and in which "crowds" and bustle have replaced face-to-face contacts and "peace and tranquillity." Should Mansfield Park model itself along these lines and make money its only source of value, it will suffer a similar loss of humanity. Like Mary Crawford's London set, the rich will become "cold-hearted" through "habits of wealth," and, like the Prices in Portsmouth, the poor will be degraded by lack of money.

Only one member of the Bertram family, the poor relation Fanny Price, has sufficient grasp of Mansfield ideals, and understanding of the relationship of manners to morals, to remain impervious to the influence of the Crawfords. Therefore, the survival of the old order depends entirely on her. Unfortunately, Fanny is in many ways ill-equipped for this task. Natural reticence, physical weakness, uncertainty about her position within the family, and exclusion from the Bertrams' social life, have combined to make Fanny an extremely timid and passive person, a "creepmouse" incapable of asserting herself in the social context. Yet unadorned virtue has little attraction for the frivolous Maria, Julia, and Tom, and soon palls even for Edmund, once he experiences the charms of Mary Crawford. Fanny's repeated attempts to be "of service" may be admirable, but, since they usually take the form of fetching and carrying for Lady Bertram and Mrs Norris, they do little more than convince the younger Bertrams that she is a kind of superior servant who can be conveniently ignored. If her morality is to become attractive to them it must be cloaked in a pleasing social performance. Only with an improvement in her manners, then, can Fanny hope to move out of the little white attic and the east room, and become guardian of the whole house, or, as [Avrom] Fleishman puts it, develop from the position of ward to that of warden.

The main business of the formal social occasion in *Mansfield Park* is to trace the way in which Fanny effects this transition in her polite performance. The process can be broken down into three stages, each of which is structured around a pattern of movement that reflects the current state of Fanny's relationship to her society. In the first part of the novel, Fanny remains passive, and is frequently left on the edge of the circle of involvement as the Bertrams move away from her and towards the Crawfords. Only Edmund introduces a variation into the pattern because he has sufficient sympathy for Fanny's morality to gravitate repeatedly towards her, before being pulled away by the force of Mary Crawford's charm. In the second part, Fanny becomes more active and by attracting others towards her, most notably Sir Thomas Bertram and Henry Crawford, is able to progress towards the centre of her social circle. In the third part, however, she must become still again, because further movement can be achieved only by giving in to attempts to make her marry Henry Crawford. The pattern of forces at work here, however, is very different from that which operated in the first part of the novel. Then Fanny was left isolated and morally impotent as others moved away from her. Now she is the centre of attention, and, if she can remain still in the face of concerted pressure to make her move, she will force Henry Crawford to expose his moral deficiencies and thus bring about the salvation of Mansfield Park.

The extent to which Fanny's lack of charm limits her sphere of moral influence becomes very evident during the first formal encounter between the Bertrams and the Crawfords. The evening's main topic of conversation is improvements, and the positions taken by the participants leave little doubt of their relative worth. The aversion which Fanny expresses towards Rushworth's plan to destroy the avenue of trees leading up to Sotherton reveals her preference for that which has developed organically over that which is drastically innovative, and thus places her solidly in the conservative tradition. Mary Crawford, who, significantly, is seated "exactly opposite" Fanny, states a willingness to accept any improvements that can be purchased, but not to endure the business of improving: "I should be most thankful to any Mr Repton who would undertake it, and give me as much beauty as he could for my money; and I should never look at it, till it was complete." As is the case here, so in general, Mary tends to assume that money rather than personal commitment is all that is needed to achieve the good things in life. Henry Crawford, on the other hand, as he admits himself, gains pleasure from the process of improvement rather than from its results. The project of improving his estate at Everingham involved him totally, but once it was completed, he lost all interest. The larger implications of Henry Crawford's attitude to improvements are defined by his own words: "My plan was laid at Westminster—a little altered perhaps at Cambridge, but at one and twenty executed. I am inclined to envy Mr Rushworth for having so much happiness yet before him. I have been a devourer of my own." In their different ways, both Mary and Henry Crawford reveal a stunted comprehension of the individual's moral relationship with time, she trying to deny that the past need play any role in shaping the present, and he involving himself totally in the present at the expense of future considerations. Only Fanny views life in the correct way as a continuum of past, present, and future.

Mary's materialism and its incompatibility with the values of the old order are further exposed during a conversation about the delivery of her harp. For Mary, the transportation of the harp from Northampton to Mansfield is a matter of business pure and simple, and should be handled by direct enquiry and by an appropriate disposition of money. In the country, however, business methods have not yet taken precedence over traditional ways of doing things, and Mary is astonished to discover that she must rely on a chain of personal connections to discover the whereabouts of her harp, and the possibility of a quick profit is not sufficient to persuade the farmers to divert their carts from the harvest. Money plays such a central part in Mary Crawford's system of values that when Edmund, doubtless inspired by recent victories over the French, describes the navy as "a noble profession," she replies: "Yes, the profession is well enough under two circumstances; if it make the fortune, and there be discretion in spending it." To this crude materialism Mary Crawford occasionally adds vulgarity, as in her joke about "*Rears, and Vices.*"

However, clear as the moral distinctions between Fanny and the Crawfords may be, they mean little to any of the Bertrams, with the partial exception of Edmund. Mary and Henry have been witty and charming; Fanny has been dull as usual. Therefore, when the question of a visit to Sotherton arises at the end of the evening, no one but Edmund disagrees with Mrs Norris's decision that Fanny would be excluded from the party. Even Edmund, however, does not go so far as to suggest that the Crawfords are not fit company for the Bertrams, and there are clear signs that for him Mary Crawford's liveliness goes a long way towards compensating for her moral deficiencies. In reviewing the conduct of the guests, Edmund begins by calling upon Fanny to confirm his view that Mary Crawford's behaviour was "very wrong—very indecorous." It is not long though before Edmund ceases to express moral outrage, and he concludes his comments by excusing what he initially condemned:

The right of a lively mind, Fanny, seizing whatever may contribute to its own amusement or that of others; perfectly allow-
able, when untinctured by ill humour or roughness; and there
is not a shadow of either in the countenance or manner of Miss
Crawford.

Patterns of movement are thus suggested in this scene which can only
intensify so long as Fanny has nothing better than passive virtue to set
against the charms of the Crawfords. Maria, Julia, and Tom will inevitably
continue to gravitate away from what is silent, still, and, to them, almost
invisible, and towards what is talkative and lively. Edmund, even though
he is by no means blind to Fanny's worth, will put an increasing value on
Mary Crawford's attractive manners. Fanny, as a result, will become ever
more isolated and thus powerless to prevent the corruption of the old order.

By the time of the Sotherton visit the patterns have achieved sharp
definition. Again, there can be little doubt that the others should look to
Fanny for guidance. Apart from Edmund, neither the visitors to Sotherton
nor its owners can begin to match Fanny's understanding of what this great
house, "built in Elizabeth's time," stands for. Rushworth and his mother
are punctilious about questions of etiquette; the guests are "welcomed by
him with due attention" and eat a lunch characterised by "abundance and
elegance." However, they have little grasp of anything more substantial.
The history of the house is something that Mrs Rushworth has learnt simply
that she might be able to guide and impress visitors, and in no sense does
she regard herself as part of a living tradition. The state of the cottages in
the village, which Maria describes as a "disgrace," the distance of the church
from the house, and the redundancy of the family chapel suggest that
Rushworth neglects both his secular and religious obligations to the community under his charge. For Maria and Julia Bertram Sotherton is, like
their own house, nothing more than a place of confinement, "a dismal old
prison," from which they must escape as soon as possible. The Crawfords
are equally unsympathetic to Sotherton; Henry wants to introduce improvements that will change its entire character, and Mary judges the tour
of the house "the greatest bore in the world." Fanny, by contrast, is eager
to learn all she can about the house and its history, and through her imagination its traditions reassume some of their former vitality: "There is
something in a chapel and chaplain so much in character with a great house,
with one's ideas of what such a household should be! A whole family
assembling regularly for the purpose of prayer, is fine!"

However the Bertrams' relationships owe more to considerations of charm than ethics, and demonstrations of moral superiority go for little with them. Fanny's attractions are so minimal compared to Henry Crawford's that the Bertram sisters scarcely acknowledge her presence. Throughout the drive to Sotherton they vie for Henry's attention, and Fanny "was not often invited to join in the conversation of the others." In the wilderness Maria seats herself between Rushworth and Henry Crawford and directs all her comments to them as if Fanny were not there. When Fanny finally forces herself into Maria's attention, by warning her of the dangers, more moral than literal, of crossing the ha-ha, she is casually dismissed: "Her cousin was safe on the other side, while these words were spoken, and smiling with all the good-humour of success, she said, 'Thank you, my dear Fanny, but I and my gown are alive and well, and so good bye.' " Because he has sufficient moral sense to recognise Fanny's worth, Edmund does not reject her so readily. Indeed, it is because of his efforts that she is included in the party, and during conversations in the chapel and on the edge of the wilderness, Edmund is united with Fanny against Mary Crawford. Yet, even though the lack of respect for family worship and the clergy expressed by Mary reveals a serious lack of correct principles, she conducts herself in so "light and lively" a manner that Edmund has no hesitation in choosing to take a "serpentine course" with her deep into the wilderness, rather than sit by the tired Fanny. With the desertion of the one person who is inclined to be sympathetic to her moral position, Fanny is "left to her solitude."

The triangle of forces in which Edmund is pulled towards Fanny by respect for her moral seriousness before yielding up to the charms of Mary Crawford comes into operation again during an evening party at Mansfield. Mary continues her attack on the clergy, this time going so far as to hint that only the prospect of an immediate living and a subsequent life of idleness could have motivated Edmund to enter such an ignoble profession. And once more she finds herself faced with the combined opposition of Fanny and Edmund. Fanny's display of good sense and firm principles is so impressive on this occasion that Edmund stays beside her even after Mary Crawford joins the main party in a glee. It is not long, however, before Mary Crawford and the glee prove to be more attractive than Fanny's raptures on the stars:

> The glee began. "We will stay till this is finished, Fanny," said
> he, turning his back on the window; and as it advanced, she had
> the mortification of seeing him advance too, moving forward
> by gentle degrees towards the instrument, and when it ceased,

> he was close by the singers, among the most urgent in requesting
> to hear the glee again.

Since Maria and Julia, as usual, have no attention to spare for Fanny, Edmund's defection again ensures her complete isolation and moral impotence: "Fanny sighed alone at the window."

Fanny is equally unsuccessful during an impromptu ball held at Mansfield Park because, after dancing twice with Edmund, she loses him to Mary Crawford and finds herself without a partner. The relative positioning of the characters during the dance further underlines that once she is deprived of Edmund's companionship, Fanny becomes isolated from the Mansfield group and is unable to influence its moral direction. Taking the dance floor as a symbol for the social world, we are presented with a tableau in which Fanny alone is placed outside the circle of involvement. Inside it extremely dangerous activities are going on unchecked, for Maria, technically Rushworth's partner, is trying to attract Henry Crawford away from Julia:

> it was while all the other young people were dancing, and she
> sitting, most unwillingly, among the chaperons at the fire . . .
> Miss Bertram did indeed look happy, her eyes were sparkling
> with pleasure, and she was speaking with great animation, for
> Julia and her partner, Mr Crawford, were close to her; they were
> all in a cluster together.

Defining Fanny's task in terms of this dance metaphor, she needs to become sufficiently attractive to be invited onto the floor. However, she must find a partner who chooses her for better reasons than those which finally motivate Tom on this occasion. By electing to dance with Fanny rather than suffer the greater evil of playing cards with Mrs Norris, Tom simply reconfirms that, to the Bertrams, she is little more than an object of convenience, and thereby stresses rather than alleviates her real isolation.

Because the salvation of Mansfield Park is so dependent on Fanny's ability to become involved in society, the theatricals must be regarded as the novel's turning point. Their immediate effect is, of course, hardly promising. Inspired by yet another intruder, the idle aristocrat, Yates, the theatricals increase existing ills and lead the Bertrams into new improprieties. By allowing himself to become involved, Edmund is particularly responsible for the atmosphere of anarchy that prevails. Initially, Edmund had joined Fanny in objecting to the theatricals. However, the prospect of acting opposite Mary Crawford finally persuades him to move away from her once again and to take a role. This "descent" "from that moral elevation which he had maintained before" gives Tom and Maria an excuse to cast off the last vestiges of restraint. Tom allows the "darling project" to occupy his entire attention, and ignores his responsibility, as senior Bertram in Sir Thomas's absence, to attend to the behaviour of his sisters; Maria pursues her flirtation with Henry Crawford so furiously that even the obtuse Rushworth becomes concerned. With Edmund's desertion, Fanny is again completely isolated and although she is acutely aware of the selfishness, impropriety, expense, bustle, and noise that characterise the theatricals, she is unable to do anything to influence the conduct of the Bertrams or the Crawfords. As usual she substitutes attempts to be useful for real involvement, but none of the generosity she displays in serving as prompter, listening to complaints, or teaching Rushworth his lines, rubs off on her companions.

What is hopeful, however, is Fanny's reaction to her isolation. Morally she has no reason to doubt the wisdom of her refusal to become involved by taking the part of the Cottager's Wife. The theatricals are an offence against Sir Thomas and his home, and the particular play, *Lovers' Vows* combines political radicalism with sexual permissiveness. Yet Fanny is troubled by her decision because, for the first time, she begins to see the necessity of participating in society. Exclusion has always been painful to Fanny, but previously she has been able to find consolation in a private world of reading, nature, and correspondence with her brother William. On this occasion, however, she is so aware that the consequence and perhaps even the love she wants so badly are reserved for those who are willing to be socially active that she is unable to shift her attention away from a pursuit in which all are included but herself:

> She alone was sad and insignificant; she had no share in any thing; she might go or stay, she might be in the midst of their noise, or retreat from it to the solitude of the East room, without being seen or missed. She could almost think any thing would have been preferable to this. Mrs Grant was of consequence; *her* good nature had honourable mention—her taste and her time were considered—her presence was wanted—she was sought for and attended, and praised; and Fanny was at first in some danger of envying her the character she had accepted.

This important change in perspective is symbolized by an episode which takes place in Fanny's room. The East room, with its books, its Romantic transparencies, and its sketch of William's ship the *Antwerp* has served throughout the novel not only as a literal place of retreat for Fanny, but as

an emblem of her private inner world. On this particular occasion, Fanny
has retired into it to escape from the thoughts of the love scene that Edmund
and Mary are to rehearse that evening. Escape, however, is not possible.
Mary and Edmund seek out Fanny and rehearse the dreaded scene in front
of her. By this symbolic means, Jane Austen underlines that Fanny has now
become too conscious of the rewards of involvement to turn away from
the social context, even when what is going on there is a source of pain to
her.

Given Fanny's new impulse towards involvement, it is not surprising
that, when it is offered her a second time, she agrees to take the part of
Cottager's Wife. By joining the theatricals, Fanny is putting herself in moral
danger. At the same time, though, she is assuming a position from which
she may be able to exert some influence. Therefore, rather than seeing Sir
Thomas's sudden return as providing Fanny with a lucky escape from
impropriety, we should perhaps consider it as depriving her of her first
opportunity to reconcile the demands of her conscience with the claims of
the group.

Fanny, however, is soon able to begin fulfilling her social ambitions.
The departure of Henry Crawford opens up a position for her at the Parsonage, where the bored Mary Crawford is eager for amusement and conversation; Maria's marriage leaves Lady Bertram in need of a companion,
a role she quickly fills; and, most important, Sir Thomas begins to acknowledge her claims to be considered a part of the family and hence to
be included more fully in its social life. When Lady Bertram and Mrs Norris
try to prevent Fanny accepting an invitation to dine with the Grants, it is
Sir Thomas who intervenes and ensures that she is allowed to attend.
Moreover, he forestalls Mrs Norris's mean-minded attempts to deny her
the carriage, thereby making certain that she goes in a style befitting a
member of his family. This crucial development in Sir Thomas's attitude
does not result from any great improvement in Fanny who, apart from a
physical blossoming, is still very much the person she was before he left
for Antigua. It is simply that Sir Thomas, wearied by his travels and financial
troubles, has become very sensitive to the value of those retiring qualities
which usually cause Fanny to be ignored.

Although Fanny's entry into society thus results more from luck than
anything else, once given her chance she is able to take advantage of it. To
be invited to social occasions in her own right is very different from tagging
along behind Edmund, and Fanny's self-confidence increases in proportion
to the increased consequence granted her. The visit of William Price, who
extends to her a love and sense of concern that she has never experienced

in the Bertram household, contributes further to the improvement in Fanny's spirits. As a result, her social performance becomes much more lively and appealing, and the pattern which characterised social gatherings in the first part of the novel alters significantly. Edmund is too entangled with Mary Crawford to respond appropriately even to a more attractive Fanny, but others, most notably Sir Thomas and Henry Crawford, pay her increasing attention. And so, having nervously entered the social circle at the Grants' dinner party, Fanny is able to move rapidly towards its centre. Her arrival there is marked by a ball held in her honour at Mansfield Park, and by Henry Crawford's marriage proposal.

Fanny's reaction to the Grants' invitation shows that she has not forgotten what she learned during the theatricals. Although she does not relish the prospect of seeing Edmund and Mary together, Fanny is fully appreciative of this rare opportunity for social involvement:

> Simple as such an engagement might appear in other eyes, it had novelty and importance in her's, for excepting the day at Sotherton, she had scarcely ever dined out before; and though now going only half a mile and only to three people, still it was dining out.

As yet, however, despite Sir Thomas's insistence that she be treated as his niece, Fanny does not have enough sense of her own importance to disagree with Mrs Norris's contention that she must be "lowest and last," and her plans for the evening involve nothing more ambitious than to "sit silent and unattended to." In the event, though, Fanny does rather better than that. Throughout dinner she takes no part in the conversation but, perhaps inspired by her new sense of belonging to the Bertram family, she is unable to remain silent when Henry Crawford laments her uncle's role in halting the theatricals:

> He seemed determined to be answered; and Fanny, averting her face, said with a firmer tone than usual, "As far as *I* am concerned, sir, I would not have delayed his return for a day. My uncle disapproved of it all so entirely when he did arrive, that in my opinion, every thing had gone quite far enough."

This brief display of intense feeling (she had never before spoken "so angrily to any one"), has a remarkable effect on Henry Crawford. Suddenly he recognises Fanny as a person of unique qualities rather than as an object to be ignored, and not only does he quickly concur with her judgment but makes several determined attempts to engage her in further conversation both then and later in the evening. Even when he is talking to Edmund, Henry's attention does not pass away entirely from Fanny: "I shall make a point of coming to Mansfield to hear you preach your first sermon . . . When is it to be? Miss Price, will not you join me in encouraging your cousin?"

Fanny's performance at the Grants' next, and much larger, dinner party is even more impressive. The rare opportunities for "unchecked, equal, fearless intercourse" provided by the visit of her brother William have produced a great improvement in her appearance and spirits, and she is much less reticent than on any previous occasion. Thus, even though she has never played Speculation before, Fanny is quite willing to take part in the game that occupies the guests after dinner, and acquits herself well enough that when she withdraws from the social circle in order to talk to William, a new circle quickly forms around her:

> The chief of the party were now collected irregularly round the fire, and waiting the final break up. William and Fanny were the most detached. They remained together at the otherwise deserted card-table, talking very comfortably and not thinking of the rest, till some of the rest began to think of them.

Although Fanny is doubtless most satisfied by the interest Sir Thomas shows in her, Henry Crawford's chair is in fact "the first to be given a direction towards" her, and it is his notice that has helped to bring her into prominence throughout the evening. By this time Henry, who has been tremendously impressed by "the glow of . . . cheek, the brightness of . . . eye" that Fanny displays when animated by William's company, is close to believing himself in love, and he pays her attention whenever possible. During the card game, for example, Henry sits next to Fanny and, by striving "to inspirit her play, sharpen her avarice, and harden her heart," magnifies delicate charms that might otherwise have gone unnoticed in the midst of such a boisterous activity as Speculation. Similarly, when the subject of improvements comes up, Henry does not allow himself to become so involved in his favourite topic as to forget to include Fanny in the conversation: "*You* think with me, I hope—(turning with a softened voice to Fanny).—Have you ever seen the place?" Later, Henry pays Fanny a polite compliment on her dancing that increases her prestige with Sir Thomas Bertram, and, at the moment of departure, places her shawl around her shoulders, with a "prominent attention."

This rapid improvement in Fanny's attitude towards and performance during social gatherings reaches its climax with the Mansfield ball, which

Sir Thomas plans almost entirely in her honour. Although she still lacks sufficient respect for herself to realise that the ball is intended to mark her "coming-out," Fanny anticipates the opportunity for social involvement with pleasure, and plans to take part in an active if limited way:

> To dance without much observation or any extraordinary fatigue, to have strength and partners for about half the evening, to dance a little with Edmund, and not a great deal with Mr Crawford, to see William enjoy himself, and be able to keep away from her aunt Norris, was the height of her ambition, and seemed to comprehend her greatest possibility of happiness.

Furthermore, the quality of her polite performance is now of sufficient importance to Fanny that she is willing to suffer Mary Crawford's company in order to get advice about her dress, and despite her disapproval of Henry Crawford, she is glad to have secured him as a voluntary partner with whom to open the ball:

> To be secure of a partner at first, was a most essential good— for the moment of beginning was now growing seriously near, and she so little understood her own claims as to think, that if Mr Crawford had not asked her, she must have been the last to be sought after, and should have received a partner only through a series of inquiry, and bustle, and interference which would have been terrible.

Clearly, Fanny has learnt the lessons of the Mansfield theatricals well, and the ball has sufficient claims in itself that not even Edmund's approval or support is necessary. Edmund is so caught up in problems of ordination and marriage that "to engage [Mary Crawford] early for the first two dances" is "the only preparation for the ball which he could enter into," and he can express no more than the limpest of enthusiasm for what is to be the most important day of Fanny's life: "Oh! yes, yes, and it will be a day of pleasure. It will all end right. I am only vexed for a moment." Yet Fanny's spirits survive Edmund's dampening effect, and the ball increasingly comes to represent "such an evening of pleasure before her!"

By granting her the privilege of opening the ball, Sir Thomas forces Fanny into a much more prominent position than she would ever have chosen. Nevertheless, she is now well enough versed in the ways of society to put on an admirable performance:

> Young, pretty, and gentle, however, she had no awkwardnesses that were not as good as graces, and there were few persons

present that were not disposed to praise her. She was attractive, she was modest, she was Sir Thomas's niece, and she was soon said to be admired by Mr Crawford. It was enough to give her general favour. Sir Thomas himself was watching her progress down the dance with much complacency: he was proud of his niece.

This triumphant opening guarantees the success of the rest of the evening. Even if anyone is still inclined to underrate Fanny's claims, Sir Thomas's open display of admiration ensures that they pay her attention. Thus, Mary Crawford recognises that it would be politic "to say something agreeable of Fanny." On the whole, though, Fanny has displayed sufficient charms for this sponsorship to be unnecessary and, far from being short of partners as she had feared, she finds she is "eagerly sought after."

Fanny's performance at the ball completes Henry Crawford's infatuation, and shortly afterwards he asks her to marry him. Acceptance of this proposal would in many ways give Fanny the social consequence she so desperately needs, since Henry Crawford is a man who, in Sir Thomas's opinion, possesses both "situation in life, fortune, and character," and "more than common agreeableness, with address and conversation pleasing to every body." However, consequence arrived at in this way would be worthless to Fanny. To marry a man whom she does not love would destroy her chances of emotional fulfilment. Furthermore, Crawford is so corrupt he would prevent Fanny exercising any moral influence on her society. The implications of a match between Henry and Fanny are made clear by a part of the conversation that takes place during the game of Speculation at the Grants'. Crawford's account of how he lost his way and stumbled upon Thornton Lacey, which is to be Edmund's living, is emblematic of his attempt to usurp Edmund's emotional and moral role in Fanny's life. Henry Crawford's inability to comprehend the new moral code with which he is striving to associate himself is clearly revealed when he outlines his plans to "improve" Thornton Lacey. These would serve, as Mary interprets them, "to shut out the church, sink the clergyman" and produce in their place "the respectable, elegant, modernized, and occasional residence of a man of independent fortune." In spite of his affection for Fanny, and his temporary leaning towards her ethical position, we can be sure that once they were married Henry would try to bring about a similar improvement in her.

By putting her heroine in this situation, Jane Austen demonstrates that the equation she has been developing between social graces and moral influence is not a simple one. As a result of the attentions paid her by Sir Thomas Bertram and Henry Crawford, Fanny has at last established a firm foothold in society. Unfortunately, her most obvious way of progressing further is to follow the "serpentine course" that would be opened up by marrying Henry. Fanny is far too wise not to be alert to the moral implications of taking such a direction and, attractive as a position of importance is to her, she is not much tempted to accept Henry's offer. However, now that she has come to the notice of her society, Fanny finds that her moral life is no longer entirely her own business. Having abandoned the sanctuary of an isolated inner life, as represented by the East room, she cannot simply retreat back into it when social involvement becomes difficult and unpleasant. Thus, Fanny's room provides her with only half-an-hour of comfort before Sir Thomas follows her into it and at once offers a reminder of the advantages of social consequence, by insisting that a fire be lit especially for her, and makes its problems very evident by questioning her right to refuse such a desirable offer. Since Sir Thomas's efforts are supported by Lady Bertram, Mary Crawford, and even Edmund, what seemed at first to be a simple moral decision turns out to be a complex issue, involving Fanny's obligations not only to herself but also to her group. Fanny has always wanted to be of service to the Bertrams and to be loved by them. Now they make it clear that not only can she achieve both goals by marrying Henry Crawford, but that failure to comply with their wishes will be interpreted as an act of ingratitude and a demonstration of lack of affection. This makes it hard for Fanny to keep in view the greater long-term good that she can do the Bertrams by refusing Henry Crawford.

In a sense, then, Fanny's position is worse than ever, because she is now being tempted and pressured to exchange her most important values for prestige, security, and wealth. However, in another, and finally more important, sense, it is better because she is at last the object of everyone's attention, and if she can remain true to her principles she will inevitably exercise a moral influence on the lives of those around her. Fanny's task, therefore, is to be still and to wait patiently until Henry Crawford either acquires the moral insight to respect her wishes or loses patience and passes on to a new interest. This stillness, which must be maintained at the centre of a world in which all around are united in their attempts to make her move, and, later, through a period of enforced exile, is clearly very different from her earlier isolated and morally impotent passivity.

There has been, then, a complete reversal in Fanny's situation. Before, she lingered on the edge of the circle of involvement and was ignored. Now, she is at the centre and her task is to ignore. This is particularly evident during an evening at Mansfield Park. When Henry Crawford conducts an impromptu reading, he does it entirely for Fanny's benefit, and she tries to deny him her attention: "Not a look, or an offer of help had Fanny given; not a syllable for or against. All her attention was for her work. She seemed determined to be interested by nothing else." This proves to be extremely difficult, however, because Henry has chosen an activity at which he is particularly skilled and in which he knows Fanny will take pleasure. Furthermore, not even the tiniest gesture of interest will go unnoticed, because Edmund is so anxious to find out the state of Fanny's feelings that he concentrates on the audience rather than the performer. For all her efforts, Fanny fails the test:

> Edmund watched the progress of her attention, and was amused and gratified by seeing how she gradually slackened in the needle-work, which, at the beginning, seemed to occupy her totally; how it fell from her hand while she sat motionless over it—and at last, how the eyes which had appeared so studiously to avoid him throughout the day, were turned and fixed on Crawford, fixed on him for minutes, fixed on him in short till the attraction drew Crawford's upon her, and the book was closed, and the charm was broken.

As a result of this lapse, Edmund becomes convinced that Crawford's attentions are welcomed, and withdraws in order to give him the chance to approach Fanny directly:

> Crawford was instantly by her side again, intreating to know her meaning; and as Edmund perceived, by his drawing in a chair, and sitting down close by her, that it was to be a very thorough attack, that looks and undertones were to be well tried, he sank as quietly as possible into a corner, turned his back, and took up a newspaper.

Failure to remain absolutely still, then, has painful consequences because it exposes Fanny to extremely violent expressions of love and claims of constancy. However, such slight movements do not make it at all likely that she will accept Henry Crawford, and the *tête-à-tête* is brought to a conclusion in a manner that reminds us of the enormous task that Crawford has set himself. When Baddely enters with the tea things, he does not just represent a convenient intervention but rather, as is suggested by the formal tones in which Jane Austen describes him, that great weight of Mansfield tradition which buttresses Fanny's value system and which she is pledged to preserve:

"The solemn procession, headed by Baddely, of tea-board, urn, and cake bearers, made its appearance." If Crawford is ever to succeed, this is what he must shift.

Given the important part played by Mansfield Park and its traditions in Fanny's rejection of Henry Crawford, Sir Thomas would seem to have made an astute move when he exiles her to Portsmouth. Without the physical presence of Mansfield to remind Fanny of what she is defending, it seems likely that she will be more easily influenced in Henry's favour. Sir Thomas, however, completely misjudges what Mansfield means to Fanny. It is his hope that the deprivations she will experience in the Price household will make Fanny more appreciative of "the elegancies and luxuries of Mansfield Park," and consequently more ready to accept a man of "good income" who can offer her such things on a permanent basis. Instead, life in Portsmouth simply makes Fanny increasingly aware of the evil consequences of yielding up Mansfield values of "consideration of times and seasons . . . regulation of subject, . . . propriety . . . attention towards every body." Portsmouth, like London, with which Fanny also becomes intimately acquainted through the steady flow of letters she receives from Mary Crawford and Edmund, is a harbinger of what things will be like after the Mansfield Parks disappear and society becomes completely urbanised. The old rural order is based on principles of order and continuity which derive directly from the natural world in which it is located. These values are thus soon lost in places where nature intrudes only in the form of the sun's "stifling, sickly glare," and in London and Portsmouth "nothing [is] of consequence but money." This discovery Fanny makes in a very personal and rather painful way because she goes to Portsmouth hoping to experience the kind of love that she has always felt the lack of at Mansfield. What she finds, however, is that, deprived of the support of the paternalistic structures which operate in a society based on human considerations, her impoverished mother has become too caught up in the business of survival to have any emotional energy to spare for her returning daughter. The kind of quiet reflection which is necessary if the individual is to go beyond concern for the self is simply not possible amidst the "noise, disorder, and impropriety" in which economic circumstances compel Mrs Price to live. Thus, although Fanny arrives in Portsmouth quite ready to sacrifice "manner" for "love," she soon comes to realise that, without manner, love is almost impossible. Mansfield's "elegance, propriety, regularity, harmony" do not guarantee that proper attention will be paid to the needs of the individual, but they do provide the conditions for such attention. In Portsmouth, the conditions simply do not exist, and the breakdown of human relationships is inevitable.

Fanny conducts several experiments in the humanising of financial transactions. A dispute over the ownership of a silver knife, for example, causes recurring disagreements between Betsey and Susan, and Fanny finds that by buying another knife she can solve the problem. Similarly, by subscribing to a circulating library, Fanny is able to contribute to Susan's liberal education. Acquaintance with the manners of London, however, teaches Fanny that, in a society founded on the cash ethic, those who have managed to accumulate excess wealth do not commonly employ it in such ways. The rich value their money not because it enables them to be of service to others, but because it confers prestige on themselves. Thus, in spite of Rushworth's limitations as a human being, Maria is envied a marriage in which she has got "her pennyworth for her penny." As a consequence of adopting such an approach to experience, people become "cold-hearted" and "vain," and Fanny is able to conclude that "the influence of London [is] very much at war with all respectable attachments."

Thus, so long as a return to Mansfield Park can be achieved only by accepting Henry Crawford, Fanny must contrive to remain still, this time in the less comfortable surroundings of the Prices' parlour. Her conviction that this is the only way of preventing Mansfield from becoming another Portsmouth or London is so firm that she remains faithful to it, even in the face of attempts by Henry Crawford to win her confidence that constitute at once the greatest performance of a man who has a chameleon ability to take on roles and the most opportunist enterprise of a man who has always lived by his wits. Although he is far too corrupt to live by Fanny's values, Crawford has sufficient moral sense to recognise what these values are, and during his visit to Portsmouth he passes himself as a very fair facsimile of the responsible country gentleman. During a walk to the Dockyard, for example, Crawford displays great consideration for the needs of Fanny, Susan, and Captain Price. Price is something of a vulgarian, but Henry Crawford treats him with extreme civility, and seeks out subjects of common interest. At the same time, he is attentive to Susan and Fanny, and ensures that they are not left to fend for themselves through the streets of Portsmouth: "at any crossing, or any crowd, when Mr Price was only calling out, 'Come girls—come, Fan—come, Sue—take care of yourselves—keep a sharp look out,' he would give them his particular attendance." The role Henry Crawford is creating is by no means an impromptu one. Thus, he has recently paid a visit to his previously neglected estate at Everingham in order that it might serve as a prop in his performance as the responsible landowner:

For her approbation, the particular reason of his going into Nor-
folk at all, at this unusual time of year, was given. It had been
real business, relative to the renewal of a lease in which the
welfare of a large and (he believed) industrious family was at
stake. . . . He had gone, had done even more good than he had
foreseen, had been useful to more than his first plan had com-
prehended, and was now able to congratulate himself upon it,
and to feel, that in performing a duty, he had secured agreeable
recollections for his own mind.

As was the case in the Mansfield drawing room, Fanny is by no means
unimpressed by the part Henry plays. At the end of his first day in Portsmouth, she judges him "altogether improved," and after he leaves "she
was quite persuaded of his being astonishingly more gentle, and regardful
of others, than formerly." Fanny, however, is too deeply imbued in the
Mansfield approach to experience, whereby the cycle of the year rather
than the moment is the basic unit of time, for such a brief performance,
sparkling though it is, to alter her feelings. Far from moving towards an
acceptance of Henry Crawford, Fanny simply hopes that as a consequence
of his new awareness of her needs he will "not much longer persevere in
a suit so distressing to her." Thus, even though Henry presses her in person
and through his sister to return to Mansfield with him, Fanny prefers to
remain in Portsmouth rather than "be owing such felicity to persons in
whose feelings and conduct . . . she saw so much to condemn."

By remaining still, Fanny demands of Henry Crawford that he display
qualities of perseverance and moral commitment that are alien to his nature
and to the world from which he derives. A situation is thus created which
almost guarantees that, so long as Fanny does not die under the harsh
conditions of life in Portsmouth, Mansfield Park will be saved. And, indeed,
Crawford's patience soon runs out, and his attention is directed back to
Maria, with whom he elopes. This elopement sets in motion a chain of
events that leads to the complete moral re-ordering of Mansfield Park.
Mary's cynical and worldly response to Henry's behaviour at last convinces
Edmund that hers are the incurable faults "of blunted delicacy and a corrupted, vitiated mind"; Sir Thomas finally becomes aware that his conduct
as a parent has been gravely deficient; and even Julia and Tom begin to
make efforts to correct their way of life. Other corrupting influences are
rapidly dispelled as Mrs Norris leaves to keep her beloved Maria company
in exile, and the Grants move to London. All that then remains is for

Edmund, free at last to recognise his cousin's charms, to fall in love with and marry Fanny Price. After a short removal to Thornton Lacey, they inevitably take their place at Mansfield Parsonage, which becomes vacant with Dr Grant's convenient death. With this restoration of spiritual significance to the very place through which the Crawfords made their entry, the moral rebirth of Mansfield Park and the salvation of the old society is completed.

Fanny's ability to resist all efforts to make her marry Henry Crawford is ultimately responsible for the regeneration of Mansfield society. However, if she had not come to realise the importance of operating within the social context, and if she had not managed to develop a more attractive polite performance, Fanny would not have been given the chance to exercise her moral strength. To make this equation between charm and moral influence clear, Jane Austen structures the formal social occasions in *Mansfield Park* around three patterns of movement, which reflect the successive stages in Fanny's relationship with her society. Fanny begins and ends in a condition of stillness, but there is a period of movement in the middle sections of the novel that makes them very different in quality. At first, Fanny's firm morality has no influence on the direction of Mansfield life because the Bertrams find her dull and repeatedly move away from her. However, by daring to become socially involved, and by learning charm, she gradually progresses to the centre of her society. Having achieved a position in which others move towards rather than away from her, she can become still again and yet exercise a moral influence. In condemning Mary Crawford, then, *Mansfield Park* does not, as is sometimes supposed, condemn vitality and charm. On the contrary, through its presentation of Fanny's development from passivity to stillness, it demonstrates that firm principles are worthless unless expressed through pleasing manners.

Feeling as One Ought about Fanny Price

Nina Auerbach

Alone among masters of fiction, Jane Austen commands the woman's art of making herself loved. She knows how to enchant us with conversational sparkle, to charm our assent with a glow of description, to entice our smiles with the coquette's practiced glee. No major novelist is such an adept at charming. Samuel Richardson, her greatest predecessor, disdained gentlemanly amenities in his revelations of the mind's interminable, intractable mixture of motives when it engages itself in duels of love; George Eliot, her mightiest successor, rejected charm as an opiate distracting us from the harsh realities her knobby, convoluted books explore. These majestic truth-tellers could not write winningly if they tried, for they are too dismally aware of the dark side of enchantment; while even in her harshest revelations, Jane Austen is a maestro at pleasing.

Yet, from the cacophony of marriages with which it begins, to the depressed union which ends it, *Mansfield Park* is unlikable. When so knowing a charmer abrades her reader, her withdrawal from our pleasure must be deliberate. She herself studied the gradations of liking *Mansfield Park* inspired, something she had not troubled to do with her earlier books, as we know from her meticulously compiled "Opinions of *Mansfield Park*": "My Mother—not liked it so well as P. & P.—Thought Fanny insipid.— Enjoyed Mrs. Norris.— . . . Miss Burdett—Did not like it so well as P. & P. Mrs. James Tilson—Liked it better than P. & P.," and so on. We do not know whether these carefully measured dollops of liking amused

From *Jane Austen: New Perspectives. Women and Literature,* n.s. 3. © 1983 by Holmes & Meier Publishers, Inc.

Jane Austen or annoyed her, but we do know that she was intrigued by the degree to which her unlikable novel was liked. Her apparent withdrawal from the reader's fellowship suggests a departure from the community and the conventions of realistic fiction toward a Romantic and a dissonant perspective. If we examine this difficult novel, with its particularly unaccommodating heroine, in relation to contemporaneous genres beyond the boundaries of realism, we may better understand Jane Austen's withdrawal from a commonality of delight.

The silent, stubborn Fanny Price appeals less than any of Austen's heroines. Perhaps because of this, she captivates more critics than they. "Nobody, I believe, has ever found it possible to like the heroine of *Mansfield Park*," Lionel Trilling intoned in 1955, and few would contradict this epitaph today. Yet Trilling goes on to apotheosize this literary wallflower, transfiguring her into a culturally fraught emblem who bears on her scant shoulders all the aches of modern secularism. Such later interpreters as Avrom Fleishman similarly embrace Fanny as emblem if not woman, wan transmitter of intricate cultural ideals. It seems that once a heroine is divested of the power to please, she is granted an import beyond her apparently modest sphere, for, unlike Jane Austen's other, more immediately appealing heroines, Fanny has been said to possess our entire spiritual history as it shapes itself through her in historical time. Elizabeth and Emma live for readers as personal presences, but never as the Romantic, the Victorian, or the Modern *Zeitgeist*. Failing to charm, Fanny is allowed in compensation to embody worlds.

But readers who have been trained to respect the culturally fraught Fanny still shy away from her as a character. Living in uncomfortable intimacy with her as we do when we read the novel, we recall Kingsley Amis's taunt that an evening with Fanny and her clergyman husband "would not be lightly undertaken." We may understand our heritage through Fanny Price, but ought we to want to dine with her? The question is important because, for theorists like George Levine, the more bravely realism departs from the commonality of fellowship, the more radically it tilts toward a monstrosity that undermines the realistic community itself. In the very staunchness of her virtue Fanny Price seems to me to invoke the monsters that deny the charmed circle of realistic fiction. Though she uses the word "ought" with unyielding authority, she evokes uncertainty and unease. Though we learn more about her life, and participate more intimately in her consciousness, than we do with Jane Austen's other heroines, the bothering question remains: How ought we to feel about Fanny Price?

Mansfield Park tilts away from commonality in part because it breaks the code established by Jane Austen's other novels. Few of us could read *Pride and Prejudice, Persuasion,* or even *Emma,* without liking the heroines enough to "travel with them," in Wayne Booth's charming phrase. *Mansfield Park* embodies a wryer literary perception, one especially congenial to Jane Austen's poetic contemporaries: the creator of Fanny Price assumes that one may live with a character one doesn't like. One motive power of Romantic poetry is the fascination of the uncongenial. In "Resolution and Independence," Wordsworth can be possessed by a deformed and virtually nonhuman leech-gatherer, although the poet is too remote from the old man to absorb a word of his exhortation; an unkempt sinner, Coleridge's Ancient Mariner, can snatch our imagination from a wedding, that great congenial sacrament of human community. These gnarled figures lure us out of fellowship to adopt the perspective of the monstrous and the marginal.

Fanny captures our imaginations in this same Romantic way, by welcoming the reader into her solitary animosity against the intricacies of the normal: "Fanny was again left to her solitude, and with no increase of pleasant feelings, for she was sorry for almost all that she had seen and heard, astonished at Miss Bertram, and angry with Mr. Crawford." The compelling, blighting power of Fanny's spectatorship at Sotherton is characteristic: morality dissolves into angry and unpleasant feelings whose intensity is an alternative to community. For while Fanny's Romanticism suggests itself in her isolating sensibility, her stylized effusions to nature, she is most Romantic in that, like Wordsworth's leech-gatherer or Coleridge's Mariner, there is something horrible about her, something that deprives the imagination of its appetite for ordinary life and compels it toward the deformed, the dispossessed.

This elevation of one's private bad feelings into a power alternate to social life associates Fanny not merely with early Romantic outcasts, but with such dashingly misanthropic hero-villains as Byron's Childe Harold, Mary Shelley's Frankenstein, and Maturin's Melmoth. Their flamboyant willfulness may seem utterly alien to this frail, clinging, and seemingly passive girl who annoys above all by her shyness, but like them, she is magnetically unconvivial, a spoiler of ceremonies. During the excursion to Sotherton, the rehearsals of *Lovers' Vows,* the game of Speculation, her baleful solitude overwhelms the company, perhaps because it expresses and exudes their own buried rancor. In families ranging from Sir Thomas Bertram's stately authoritarianism to the casual disorder of her father's house, Fanny exists like Frankenstein as a silent, censorious pall. Her denying spirit defines itself best in assertive negatives: "No, indeed, I cannot act."

Fanny's credo resonates beyond her particular disapproval of staging

Lovers' Vows, for, even when the play is not in question, Fanny refuses to act. Instead, and consistently, she counteracts; a creed which seems a high-minded elevation of her own honesty against the dangerous deceit of role-playing is also resistance to the comic, collective rhythms of realistic fiction itself. The joyless exercises of her delicate body tacitly condemn not only acting, but activity in general; Mary Crawford's elation at horseback riding is as antagonistic to Fanny as is her flair for acting. At Sotherton, Fanny stations herself beside the dangerous ha-ha as a still bulwark against the mutual serpentine pursuit of the other characters; playing Speculation, she alone will not take the initiative that will advance the game. Fanny's refusal to act is a criticism not just of art, but of life as well. Her timidly resolute denial of acting includes activity and play, those impulses of comedy which bring us together in ceremonial motions where fellowship seems all. Her refusals are her countercharm against the corporate and genial charm with which Jane Austen's comedies win love.

Fanny's role as counteractive genius and spirit of anti-play is anomalous in a romantic heroine, but not in a hero-villain. Like Frankenstein and his monster, those spirits of solitude, Fanny is a killjoy, a blighter of ceremonies and divider of families. It is precisely this opposition to the traditional patterns of romantic comedy that lends her her disturbing strength. Her misery amid the bustle of the play is the stigma of her power:

> She was full of jealousy and agitation. Miss Crawford came with looks of gaiety which seemed an insult, with friendly expressions towards herself which she could hardly answer calmly. Every body around her was gay and busy, prosperous and important, each had their object of interest, their part, their dress, their favourite scene, their friends and confederates, all were finding employment in consultations and comparisons, or diversion in the playful conceits they suggested. She alone was sad and insignificant; she had no share in any thing; she might go or stay, she might be in the midst of their noise, or retreat from it to the solitude of the East room, without being seen or missed.

But though she is stricken in the midst of play, unable and unwilling to act, Fanny never retreats from activity. Finally, her "jealousy and agitation" seem to take concrete shape in the angry intruder, Sir Thomas Bertram, who lends authority to Fanny's bad feelings and ends the play. Sir Thomas's interruption seems only the culmination of Fanny's silent, withering power over performance, for before he appears she has already drawn control to her watching self. Backstage, she alone is in possession of each actor's secret grievance; watching and prompting from her isolation, she alone knows everybody's lines. A center of fierce inactivity, Fanny broods jealously over the play until she masters both its script and the secret designs of its actors, at which point Sir Thomas's return vindicates her silent obstructive power. Fanny abdicates from stardom to assume a more potent control over the action: she appropriates to her solitude the controlling omniscience of the rapt audience.

As her novel's sole and constant watcher, the controlling spirit of anti-play, Fanny relinquishes performing heroism to become the jealous reader, whose solitary imagination resurrects the action and keeps it alive. In her own delicately assertive phrase, "I was quiet, but I was not blind." As quietly seeing spectator of others' activities, Fanny plays a role as ambiguous as the reader's own: like Fanny, we vivify the action by our imaginative participation in it, while we hold as well the power to obstruct it by our censure. The anomalous position of the watcher more than justifies Mary Crawford's perplexed question: "Pray, is she out, or is she not?" Withholding herself from play, Fanny ingests the play of everyone she silently sees. As omniscient spectator of all private and public performances, Fanny remains "out" of the action, while her knowledge seeps into its subtlest permutations. Our discomfort at her, then, may incorporate our discomfort at our own silent voyeurism; as a portrait of the reader as a young woman, she is our unflattering if indelible reflection. Her fierce spectatorship forces our reluctant identification.

As omniscient watcher and anti-comic spirit linked in uncomfortable community to the solitary reader, Fanny possesses a subtler power than we find in brighter and livelier heroines of fiction. That dynamic mis-reader Emma Woodhouse is forced by her own misconstructions into the limited position of actor in the comedy she is trying to control from without, while Fanny's role as omniscient outsider thrives on her continued abstention. In her role as controlling, anti-comic watcher, Fanny moves beyond the sphere of traditional heroism to associate herself with a host of dashing British villains. Like them, this denying girl will not, perhaps cannot, eat; her abstinence makes her a spectral presence at the communal feast. Reunited with her family at Portsmouth, instead of feasting with them, as any of Dickens's or Charlotte Brontë's waifs would gladly do, she is repelled by the very suggestion of food, by "the tea-board never thoroughly cleaned, the cups and saucers wiped in streaks, the milk a mixture of motes floating in thin blue, and the bread and butter growing every minute more greasy than even Rebecca's hands had first produced it." Family food induces only a strangely modern nausea. Fanny's revulsion against food, along with her psychic feasting on the activities of others, crystallizes her somewhat sinister position as outsider who strangely and silently moves into the interior. Her starved incapacity to eat familial food is suggestive of that winsome predator the vampire, an equally solitary and melancholy figure who haunts British literature in his dual role as dark abstainer from a comic dailiness of which he is secretly in possession. Like Fanny, the vampire cannot eat the common nourishment of daily life, but he feasts secretly upon human vitality in the dark.

In adopting the role of traditional literary villains, Fanny infects our imaginations in a way that no merely virtuous heroine could do. Her hungry exclusion seems unappeasable and triumphant. Insofar as she draws sustenance from her role as omniscient outsider at family, excursion, wedding, play, or feast, she stands with some venerable monsters in the English canon. Not only does she share the role of Mary Shelley's creature, that gloomy exile from family whose vocation is to control families and destroy them, but there is a shadow on her even of the melancholy Grendel in the Anglo-Saxon epic *Beowulf*. An exile from common feasting, Grendel peers jealously through the window of a lighted banquet hall. He defines his identity as outsider by appropriating the interior; he invades the lighted hall and begins to eat the eaters. At the end of *Mansfield Park,* Fanny too has won a somewhat predatory victory, moving from outsider in to guiding spirit of the humbled Bertram family. Fanny's cannibalistic invasion of the lighted, spacious estate of Mansfield is genteel and purely symbolic, but, like the primitive Grendel, she replaces common and convivial feasting with a solitary and subtler hunger that possesses its object. In this evocation of an earlier literary tradition, Fanny is Jane Austen's most Romantic heroine, for she is part of a literature newly awakened to ancient forms and fascinated by the monstrous and marginal. In the subtle streak of perversity that still disturbs readers today, she shows us the monsters within Jane Austen's realism, ineffable presences who allow the novels to participate in the darker moods of their age.

Fanny's jealous hunger, which can be assuaged only by private, psychic feasting, isolates her in comedy while it associates her with such venerable predators as the Ancient Mariner, the vampire, the Byronic hero–villain, and, in a far-off echo, *Beowulf's* Grendel. Her initiation is not that of the usual heroine, whose marriage reconciles us to the choreography of comedy; instead, like the hero–villain, she proclaims her uniqueness through possessive spectatorship. The implications of Fanny's refusal to act are more richly glossed in Romantic poetry and fiction than in early nineteenth-century realism, but Romantic criticism also illuminates the complex genesis of a Fanny Price: her stubborn creed, "I cannot act," recalls some problematic characters of Shakespeare, in whom such critics as Coleridge and Hazlitt discovered new significance.

Like *Mansfield Park,* Shakespearean drama characteristically pivots upon the performance of a play within a play; like Jane Austen, Shakespeare increasingly pushes to center stage the character who refuses to act. Thus, in his early *A Midsummer Night's Dream,* all the rustics lumber through their parts in the thoroughly comic "Pyramus and Thisbe," but by the time we reach *Twelfth Night,* the play is marred: the austere Malvolio is made to perform in a cruel drama not of his making, posturing for the delectation of the raucous plotters just as he thinks he is being most sincere. This humiliation of an upright, if unlikable, character by the cruelty of play anticipates the complex tone of *Mansfield Park,* though Fanny's sharper eye for traps forbids her seduction by the players.

Malvolio abandons his part in outrage, bellowing as he exits, "I'll be revenged on the whole pack of you!" Perhaps in his revenge he returns as Hamlet, our most famous star who refuses to act. Like Fanny, Hamlet casts himself as a jealous and melancholy death's head in a gay, if false, company. His stern creed—"Madam, I know not seems"—epitomizes, like hers, refusal to act. Nonactive in the complex political drama of his family life, Hamlet likewise takes no part in the microcosmic play within the play, though, like Fanny, he hovers hungrily around its periphery, knowing all the parts. His avid spectatorship ultimately upstages the actors and spoils the performance, replacing communal play with rage and slaughter; at the end of her novel, Fanny too reigns at Mansfield in consequence of a family havoc begun at the ruin of the play.

Of course, Fanny is not Hamlet, nor was she meant to be. She is not a doomed prince, but a pauper, a woman, and a survivor; she neither rages nor soliloquizes, revealing her power and her plans only haltingly and indirectly. Still, in her complex relation to the play which epitomizes her novel's action, Fanny has more in common with Hamlet than she does with the helpless women he excoriates when they cross his path. For Hamlet is Shakespeare's supreme anti-actor and counteractor, the avid and omniscient spectator of the game, who fascinates us as Fanny does because he expresses his virtue by the characteristics of conventional villainy. Jane Austen's contemporaries were obsessed by this troubling sort of hero: Samuel Taylor Coleridge reconceived Hamlet as a paragon of nonactivity, deifying for the modern age a character too pure to act, whose doom and calling are the destruction of play. Fanny Price may be one feminized expression of this new, Romantic fascination with Hamlet as a modern type. As Jane Austen's

Hamlet, scourge and minister of a corrupted world, the perfection of the character who won't play, Fanny Price in her unyielding opposition, her longing for a purified and contracted world, gains majesty if not charm. She is as sternly denying as Hamlet, banishing in turn her cousins Maria and Julia, her parents, and the rakish, witty Crawfords from her own finer sphere. These multiple banishments align her with one type of Romantic hero, while denying her the warmth readers want in a heroine. Confronted with so richly disturbing a figure, we would insult her to sentimentalize her when *Mansfield Park* itself does not. For, as we shall see, Fanny's anti-human qualities are stressed in the text of the novel as well as in its contexts. In her progress toward power, her charmlessness only increases her efficacy as Mansfield's scourge and minister.

"Nobody falls in love with Fanny Price," Tony Tanner warns us. We have seen that few readers have done so; Jane Austen further confounds our emotions by making clear that none of the characters within the novel falls in love with her either, though most heroines exist to win love. She wins neither the affection nor the interest of her parents, though they are not always unresponsive; the charm of a Henry Crawford evokes an answering charm in them, but when Fanny's penitential visit to Portsmouth is over at last, her parents seem as relieved to see her leave as she is to go. Kinship is equally unappetizing to all.

Within Mansfield, the gracious adoptive family to which Fanny returns with such ardor, she wins love in proportion to her cousins' shame, receiving emotional interest they failed to earn. Fanny, despised by all, is embraced as a last resource when Sir Thomas's natural children disgrace themselves in turn. Jane Austen is coolly explicit about the cannibalistic undercurrents of this, and perhaps of all, requited love:

> My Fanny indeed at this very time, I have the satisfaction of knowing, must have been happy in spite of every thing. She must have been a happy creature in spite of all that she felt or thought she felt, for the distress of those around her . . . and happy as all this must make her, she would still have been happy without any of it, for Edmund was no longer the dupe of Miss Crawford.
>
> It is true, that Edmund was very far from happy himself. He was suffering from disappointment and regret, grieving over what was, and wishing for what could never be. She knew it was so, and was sorry; but it was with a sorrow so founded on satisfaction, so tending to ease, and so much in harmony with

every dearest sensation, that there are few who might not have
been glad to exchange their greatest gaiety for it.

In this redemption from her usual depression, Fanny's only available happy
ending is the predator's comedy; surely there is deliberate irony in Jane
Austen's pitiless repetition of "happy" amid this household of collapsed
hopes. Never in the canon is the happy ending so reliant upon the wounds
and disappointments of others; though we leave Fanny ministering avidly
to these wounds, they will never heal. The love she wins from her adoptive
family is not a free tribute to her beauty, her character, or her judgment,
but the last tender impulse of a stricken household.

The love of her two suitors, Henry and Edmund, is similarly under-
mined. Everything about Henry Crawford, that mobile and consummate
actor, calls his sincerity into question. He stages his love scenes before select
audiences, all carefully chosen to put the greatest possible pressure on Fanny,
only to humiliate her flamboyantly by his elopement with Maria once she
has begun to respond. As Fanny and we know, his passion for her repeats
more grandly his pattern of behavior with her silly cousins, so that only
the most sentimentally credulous reader could find this new performance
credible. The watcher Fanny knows his love is play, and thus by definition
the medium of her humiliation; but in exposing the ardor of the romantic
hero as a sadistic game, Jane Austen undermines the reader's own impulse
to fall in love with Fanny by undermining love itself.

Readers of *Sense and Sensibility, Pride and Prejudice,* and *Emma* expect
Edmund Bertram, Fanny's proper husband and sober soulmate, to redress
the balance; the probity of this good suitor's love should define the sham
of Henry's. But if for Henry love is another variant of private theatricals,
a series of ritual attitudes staged for an audience, Edmund's love is so
restrained as to be imperceptible. Like Mr. Knightley, he is exemplary as
Fanny's tender mentor, proud of his pupil's right feelings and right attitudes,
but he has none of Mr. Knightley's life as an incipient lover. Sexual jealousy
fuels the latter's sternly protective manner and his indignant disapproval of
Frank Churchill, while Edmund hints of no passions beyond what we see,
showing not a glimmer of jealousy when Henry Crawford makes de-
monstrative love to Fanny. Edmund's impeccably clerical conscience interprets his future wife's prospective marriage as a convenience to facilitate
his own engagement to Henry's seductive sister. Jane Austen is a sharp
observer of men struggling with powerful feelings; like Knightley, Darcy
and Wentworth fight to repress, through prudence or anger, a love that
proves too strong for them; but she withholds from Edmund Bertram any

feelings worth denying. The unlocated and undramatized conversion that leads to his marriage carries as little emotional weight as it could do: "I only intreat every body to believe that exactly at the time when it was quite natural that it should be so, and not a week earlier, Edmund did cease to care about Mary Crawford, and became as anxious to marry Fanny, as Fanny herself could desire."

This clipped, perfunctory summary, together with the fact that no earlier hints have prepared us for an outbreak of passion on Edmund's part, seems deliberately designed to banish love from our thoughts. The final marriage is as stately and inevitable as Edmund's ordination will be; the ritual is performed, though neither love nor guardianship quite joins the marrying couple. The narrator's reiterated appeal to nature—"what could be more natural than the change?"—is a further symptom of the hopelessness of love, for, as we shall see below, nature is a feeble contender in the manipulated world of *Mansfield Park*. Though Edmund marries the woman he ought, the stern hope he husbands is a loveless strength.

A romance from a writer of marriage comedies that so unremittingly denies love to its heroine is a brave novel indeed, particularly when this heroine is ready to love both her emotionally desiccated suitors. If two wooing men cannot manage to love Fanny, with the true suitor proving as hollow as the false, then surely the reader never will. Austerely alone in a community of fictional heroines for whom love is their chief talent and reward, Fanny is further isolated from affection by her radical homelessness. This waiflike attribute may lead us to associate *Mansfield Park* with such Victorian orphan-myths as *Jane Eyre:* Jane, like Fanny, is an unprepossessing orphan, "a discord" in her corrupted foster family, who grows into an iron-willed little savior. But like most of her orphaned analogues in Victorian fiction, Jane is baptized into strength by the recovery of family: it is not her love for Rochester, but her healing interlude with her recovered cousins, the Rivers family, that allows her identity and her destiny to cohere. The more radical Fanny similarly recovers her family during a romantic crisis, only to discover her total absence of kin. Her ideal home is her utter homelessness. She belongs everywhere she is not: "When she had been coming to Portsmouth, she had loved to call it her home, had been fond of saying that she was going home; the word had been very dear to her; and so it still was, but it must be applied to Mansfield. *That* was now the home. Portsmouth was Portsmouth; Mansfield was home."

The word may be very dear, but the thing eludes her as she eludes it. Victorian orphan-fiction typically begins with the loss of home and ends with its recovery, but here, home is palpable to Fanny only by its absence.

Mansfield itself is no true home. The vacuum at its heart is evident not only in the flights of all its members except the supine Lady Bertram, but in the chilling ease with which it can be transformed into a theater. Upon her return, Fanny compels the gutted Mansfield to be her home by an act of will, but in its shrunken regenerate state it bears little resemblance to the place in which she grew up. Fanny's dual returns, to her natural and then to her adoptive origins, prove only the impossibility of self-discovery through return. Thus, though she may resemble later orphan-heroes, Fanny is a more indigestible figure than these wistful waifs, for whom embracing their kin is secular salvation. In the tenacity with which she adheres to an identity validated by no family, home, or love, she denies the vulnerability of the waif for the unlovable toughness of the authentic transplant. Her fragility cloaks the will to live without the traditional sanctions for life. Underlying her pious rigidity is a dispossession so fundamental that, among nineteenth-century English novelists, only the tact of a Jane Austen could dare reveal it in a lady.

Readers are right, then, to find Fanny a relentlessly uncomfortable figure in a domestic romance and to wonder nervously where Jane Austen's comedy went. This uncompromising novel never dissolves its heroine's isolation; she merely passes from the isolation of the outcast to that of the conqueror. Her solitude is rarely alleviated by pathos; instead, she hones it into a spectator's perspective from which she can observe her world and invade it. In this above all, she is closer to the Romantic hero than to the heroine of romance: her solitude is her condition, not a state from which the marriage comedy will save her. In her relentless spectatorship, Fanny may be Jane Austen's domestic answer to Byron's more flamboyant and venturesome Childe Harold, exile from his kind, passing eternally through foreign civilizations in order to create elegies to their ruins. Though Fanny travels only to Sotherton and Portsmouth, her role too is alien and elegiac, as it is at Mansfield itself; like Byron's persona, she is a hero because she is sufficiently detached to see the death of worlds. Fabricating an identity from uprootedness, she conquers the normal world that acts, plays, and marries, through her alienation from it. In the text of her novel, she is a being without kin, but in its context, she exudes a quiet kinship with the strangers and the monsters of her age.

Like other literary monsters, Fanny is a creature without kin who longs for a mate of her own kind. The pain of her difference explains a longing in *Mansfield Park* that is common to much Romantic literature and that, in its obsessed exclusiveness, may look to modern readers unnervingly like incest: the hunger of sibling for sibling, of kin for kind. Seen in its time,

the ecstatic, possessive passion Fanny divides between her brother William
and her foster brother Edmund, her horror at the Crawfords' attempt to
invade her emotions, seem less relevant to the Freudian family romance
than to the monster's agonized attempts to alleviate his monstrosity. Mary
Shelley's monster asks only that Frankenstein create for him a sister-wife;
Bram Stoker's Dracula experiences his triumphant climax when turning
his victims into fellow members of the Undead, thus making of them sisters
as well as spouses. Fanny yearns similarly in isolation for a brother-mate,
repelling the Crawfords above all because they are so different as to constitute virtually another species: "We are so totally unlike . . . we are so
very, very different in all our inclinations and ways, that I consider it as
quite impossible we should every be tolerably happy together, even if I
could like him. There never were two people more dissimilar. We have not
one taste in common. We should be miserable."

This rage of self-removal extends itself to Mary Crawford as well,
above all perhaps in the emotional spaciousness with which Mary reaches
out to Fanny as her "sister." Mary's quest for sisters of gender rather than
family, her uncomfortably outspoken championship of abused wives, her
sexual initiative, and her unsettling habit of calling things by their names,
all suggest the pioneering sensibility of her contemporary, Mary Wollstonecraft; but Fanny cannot endure so universal an embrace, clutching only
the shreds of kinship. The novel ends as it ought, with Mary's expulsion
into a wider and sadder world, while Fanny, still isolated, clings jealously
to her conquered family.

Fanny as Romantic monster does not dispel our discomfort in reading
Mansfield Park, but may explain some of it. Until recently, critics have
limited their recognition of the monsters that underlie Jane Austen's realism
to the peripheral figures whose unreason threatens the heroine, while the
heroine herself remains solidly human. Yet Fanny excites the same mixture
of sympathy and aversion as does Frankenstein's loveless, homeless creature, and the pattern of her adventures is similar to his. Frankenstein's
monster begins as a jealous outcast, peering in at family and civic joys. His
rage for inclusion makes him the hunted prey of those he envies, and he
ends as the conqueror of families. Fanny too is a jealous outcast in the first
volume. In the second, she is besieged by the family that excluded her in
the form of Henry Crawford's lethal marriage proposal; finally her lair, the
chilly East room, is hunted down like Grendel's and invaded by Sir Thomas
himself. In the third volume, Fanny, like Mary Shelley's monster, becomes
the solitary conqueror of a gutted family. This movement from outcast
within a charmed circle to one who is hunted by it and then conqueror of

it aligns Jane Austen's most Romantic, least loved heroine with the kin she so wretchedly seeks.

Modern readers may shun Fanny as a static, solitary predator, but in the world of *Mansfield Park* her very consistency and tenacity are bulwarks against a newly opening space that is dangerous in its very fluidity: even Sir Thomas Bertram's solid home is made vulnerable by economic fluctuations in far-off Antigua. Though the large and loveless house that gives it its name has made many readers feel that *Mansfield Park* is Jane Austen's most oppressive novel, its dominant emotional atmosphere induces a certain vertigo, evident in the apparent rocklike solidity, but the true and hopeless elusiveness, of the word "ought." "Ought" tolls constantly, its very sound bringing a knell of absolutism, and nobody uses it with more assurance than the hero and heroine. Fanny can dismiss Henry Crawford simply because "he can feel nothing as he ought," while Edmund freights the word with religious and national authority: "as the clergy are, or are not what they ought to be, so are the rest of the nation." As a barometer of feelings, morals, and institutions, the word seems an immutable touchstone, but in fact it has no objective validation. Its authority in the novel is entirely, and alarmingly, self-generated. The great houses Mansfield and Sotherton scarcely institutionalize the "ought" that resounds in the novel's language; the Portsmouth of the Prices and the London of the Crawfords are equally ignorant of its weight. It has no echo in the world of households and institutions.

Yet this lack of official authority does not prevent the novel's misguided characters from using the word with the same assurance as Fanny and Edmund do. Sir Thomas says of a Fanny who is brewing rebellion, "She appears to feel as she ought"; for Mary, the party with which Maria Rushworth inaugurates her miserable marriage finds everything "just as it ought to be"; Maria herself avoids only the word in seeing her mercenary marriage as "a duty." Even Edmund, who has transmitted its value to Fanny, abuses the word throughout the novel, beginning with his myopic pressure on Fanny to live with her hated Aunt Norris: "She is choosing a friend and companion exactly where she ought." The incoherence underlying Edmund's authoritative vocabulary tells us that the word recurs anarchically, for there is no objective code to endow it with consistency. Fanny, for example, longs for a loving reunion with her indifferent mother, hoping that "they should soon be what mother and daughter ought to be to each other," but as usual the novel provides no objective image of this "ought": in *Mansfield Park* and throughout Jane Austen's canon, mothers and daughters are at best indifferent and at worst antagonistic, depriving the commanding word of validation. Fanny is repeatedly hymned as the only character who feels consistently as she ought, but in a world where the word changes its meaning so incessantly, her role as a walking "ought" merely isolates her further. Whatever authority Fanny has comes magically from herself alone. Though she can control the inchoate outside world, it is too lacking in definition to claim kinship with her. `

For though Fanny possesses a quasi-magical power over the action, she represents less a moral than a shaping principle, assuming the author's prerogatives along with the reader's: the novel's action happens as she wills, and so her emotions become our only standard of right. In its essence, the world of *Mansfield Park* is terrifyingly malleable. Jane Austen detaches herself from her Romantic contemporaries to reveal both inner and outer nature as pitifully ineffectual compared to what can be made. Mrs. Price grows listless toward Fanny because the "instinct of nature was soon satisfied, and Mrs. Price's attachment had no other source." The gap between Mrs. Price and Mrs. Bertram can never heal because "where nature had made so little difference, circumstances [had] made so much." Mary Crawford's nature, like Maria's and Julia's, is similarly helpless against the constructive, or the deconstructive, power of her medium: "For where, Fanny, shall we find a woman whom nature had so richly endowed?—Spoilt, spoilt!—." By contrast, we know that Susan Price will survive, not because of her natural qualities, but because she is "a girl so capable of being made, every thing good." Nature's insufficiency may explain the deadness of Fanny's effusions to stars, trees, and "verdure," for though she laments improvements, Fanny is the most potent of the novel's improving characters. In so malleable and so defective a world, Fanny is polite to the stars, but she turns her most potent attention on the vulnerable, that which is "capable of being made."

In Mary Shelley's *Frankenstein* as well, family, nature, and even the Alps pall before the monster who is capable of being made. The monstrosity of *Mansfield Park* as a whole is one manifestation of its repelled fascination with acting, with education, and with landscape and estate improvements: the novel imagines a fluid world, one with no fixed principles, capable of awesome, endless, and dangerous manipulation. The unconvivial stiffness of its hero and heroine is their triumph: by the end, they are so successfully "made" by each other that he is her creature as completely as she has always been his. The mobility and malleability of *Mansfield Park* is a dark realization of an essentially Romantic vision, of which Fanny Price represents both the horror and the best hope. Only in *Mansfield Park* does Jane Austen force us to experience the discomfort of a Romantic universe presided over by the potent charm of a charmless heroine who was not made to be loved.

Feminist Irony and the Priceless Heroine of *Mansfield Park*

Margaret Kirkham

"I do not quite know what to make of Miss Fanny. I do not understand her." So says Henry Crawford. What to make of Miss Fanny is the central moral puzzle Jane Austen presents to her anti-hero. He fails to discover the correct solution. It is also the central puzzle presented to the reader, testing the soundness of his moral attitudes and the quickness of his wits. It may be that the author misjudged what could be expected of her readers, for they have not, by and large, solved the riddle of Miss Price satisfactorily. Even Henry Austen took a bit of time over it. He had the advantage of familiarity with contemporary works to which allusion is made, as well as a knowledge of the author's point of view, and yet he found this puzzle a difficult one. No wonder, then, that later readers, lacking his privileged knowledge, have sometimes blundered.

In this essay, I shall try to show that Jane Austen teases us about Miss Fanny. Irony, far from being suspended in *Mansfield Park,* is turned upon the reader. We are given a heroine who, in some respects, looks like an exemplary conduct-book girl, but this is deceptive. Fanny is not a true conduct-book heroine and, insofar as she resembles this ideal—in her timidity, self-abasement, and excessive sensibility, for example—her author mocks her—and us, if we mistake these qualities for virtue. Jane Austen hated "unmixed" characters in general, and "unmixed" heroines in particular, a point on which she disagreed with the Dr. Johnson of *Rambler 4.* Writing to her niece Fanny Knight (the one with a weakness for Evangelical

From *Jane Austen: New Perspectives. Women and Literature,* n.s. 3. © 1983 by Holmes & Meier Publishers, Inc.

gentlemen), she discusses the opinions of an aptly named Mr. Wildman, who had not found her novels to his taste:

> Do not oblige him to read any more.—Have mercy on him.
> . . . He and I should not in the least agree of course in our ideas about Heroines; pictures of perfection as you know make me sick and wicked—but there is some very good sense in what he says, and I particularly respect him for wishing to think well of all young Ladies; it shows an amiable and delicate Mind—And he deserves better than to be obliged to read any more of my Works.

If Jane Austen created a conduct-book heroine, it cannot have been without an ironic intention of some kind. A clue to what it was occurs in an unsigned article on the "Female Novelists" published in *New Monthly Review* in 1852: "Then again, in *Mansfield Park,* what a bewitching 'little body' is Fanny Price." This Victorian writer sees in Fanny, not a paragon of virtue, but a little enchantress, and it is important to notice that, when Crawford falls in love, he too sees her in this way. Fanny's apparent saintliness is closely connected with her sexual desirableness, as Crawford shows in chapter 12 of the second volume, where he tells his sister that he is in love. His appreciation of "Fanny's graces of manner and goodness of heart," as well as his recognition of her "being well-principled and religious," is mingled with his dwelling on her "charms," "her beauty of face and figure," her beautifully heightened color, as she attends to the service of that stupid woman, her Aunt Bertram, and the neat arrangement of her hair, with "one little curl falling forward . . . which she now and then shook back."

Crawford is incapable of understanding that the "religious principles" he admires in Fanny are formed, as Providence intended rational beings to form moral principles, out of rational reflection upon experience. His view of her is deeply sentimental, for he sees her as something like the ideal woman of Rousseau's *Émile,* innocent, virtuous, tractable, and crying out for protective love, which her prettiness and gentleness excite in him. By volume 3, he discovers that she has "some touches of the angel" in her. Henry Austen must have seen at that point, if he had not seen it before, that his sister would not allow her heroine to marry Crawford, for Austen's objection to the comparison of young women to angels is so consistently maintained that this blunder of Crawford's could not pass unnoticed. Elizabeth Bennet once says, jokingly and critically, that her sister Jane has angelic characteristics (*Pride and Prejudice*); otherwise, from the *Juvenilia* to the mature works, only fools or villains make this analogy. It is pointedly avoided by all the Austen heroes, but used to define the defects of the more complex anti-heroes, notably Willoughby and Crawford, and to define Emma's disillusion with Frank Churchill (*Emma*).

The point is of great importance to a right understanding of Fanny Price and *Mansfield Park,* because it directs us to the criticism of the conduct-book ethos which is the essential irony of Miss Price's characterization. It may seem strange to us that physical weakness, or lassitude, should be thought to enhance a girl's sexual attractiveness, nor do we think religiosity alluring, but it was not always so. The conduct-book ideal of young womanhood was deeply sentimental, and the genre included works in which salaciousness was mixed with moral advice.

Two examples, quoted and proscribed by Mary Wollstonecraft in *A Vindication of the Rights of Woman,* are of especial interest. Wollstonecraft berates James Hervey, whose *Meditations and Contemplations,* written between 1745 and 1746, were "still read" in 1792. Hervey told his readers (mostly female) that:

> Never, perhaps, does a fine woman strike more deeply, than when, composed into pious recollection, and possessed with the noblest considerations, she assumes, without knowing it, superior dignity and new graces; so that the beauties of holiness seem to radiate about her, and the bystanders are almost induced to fancy her already worshipping among the kindred angels.

Mary Wollstonecraft could not stand that sort of thing. "Should," she asks, "a grave preacher interlard his discourses with such folleries? . . . Why are girls to be told that they resemble angels: but to sink them below women." Like Jane Austen, she has no patience either with Dr. Fordyce, whose *Sermons to Young Women* (1766) contain a remarkable passage in which the awfulness of abusing young angels is discussed with salacious relish:

> Behold these smiling innocents, whom I have graced with my fairest gifts, and committed to your protection; behold them with love and respect; treat them with tenderness and honour. They are timid and want to be defended. They are frail; oh do not take advantage of their weakness! Let their fears and blushes endear them. Let their confidence in you never be abused. But is it possible, that any of you can be such barbarians, so supremely wicked, as to abuse it? Can you find in your hearts to despoil the gentle, trusting creatures of their treasure, or do anything to strip them of their native robe of virtue? Curst be

the impious hand that would dare to violate the unblemished form of chastity! Thou wretch! thou ruffian! forbear; nor venture to provoke Heaven's fiercest vengeance.

Mary Wollstonecraft says, not unreasonably:

I know not any comment that can be made seriously on this curious passage, and I could produce many similar ones; and some, so very sentimental, that I have heard rational men used the word indecent when they mentioned them with disgust.

It will be remembered that it was Fordyce's *Sermons* that Mr. Collins chose, after having turned down a novel, to read aloud to the ladies at Longbourn. Perhaps it was at just such a passage that Lydia Bennet, no angel, but "a stout well-grown girl of fifteen," interrupted his "monotonous solemnity" to tell her mother an interesting bit of gossip about the regiment quartered nearby. At all events, Mr. Collins's approbation of Fordyce is a clear indication that Jane Austen disapproved of him.

There is good reason to think, in the light of her novels and letters, that this was a disapproval founded in sympathy with rational, post-Enlightenment feminism. This is not to suggest that Austen was in agreement with Wollstonecraft on anything more than these fundamental ideas: (a) that women, being possessed of the same "powers of mind" as men, have the same moral status and the same moral accountability; (b) that girls should be educated in a manner appropriate to this view of the female sex; (c) that a "respectable" marriage is an "equal" marriage, in which man and woman are "partners," and must therefore rest on "friendship and esteem," and (d) that literary works in which any other view is endorsed are objectionable. Modern feminists may find these very tame, but around 1800 they were the essential convictions of rational feminism. We need not be put off because Austen is "a moralist" after the Johnsonian fashion; so, in many respects, is Wollstonecraft, especially in the *Vindication,* itself a sort of conduct book. The moral argument upon which Wollstonecraft bases her feminist case derives very largely from Bishop Butler's *Analogy of Religion* (1796) and from Richard Price's *Review of the Central Question in Morals* (1758). Butler was a bishop of the established church, whose views accord to a large extent with Johnson's. Price was a Dissenter and, through his influence upon progressive Dissent, associated not only with Wollstonecraft herself but with many of the radicals of his time. His ambience was thus quite different from Butler's, but the essential character of his view of morals was not, as he himself acknowledges.

So far as late-eighteenth-century feminism went, Butler and Price could both be seen as laying down principles upon which a feminist moralist could found her argument. This is crucial to a right understanding of the relationship between the first well-known English feminist theorist, Mary Wollstonecraft, and the first major woman novelist in English. Thinking of them, as we do, as totally different in their religious and political affiliations, lifestyle, and temperament, we may easily miss what connects them as feminist moralists, whose roots lie in a common tradition of ethical discussion. There is no need to assume that Austen was an undercover Jacobin because she is so close to Wollstonecraft as a feminist moralist.

Austen's implicit demand that men and women be judged, and judge themselves, by the same, somewhat strict, standard in sexual matters, should not be seen as a sign of her commitment to anti-Jacobin fervor. It is no more than the mark of her convinced feminism. Among the radicals, as both Gary Kelly and Marilyn Butler show, feminist feeling went hand in hand with emphasis upon the need for reason and restraint in sexual matters. Butler is impatient with them about it: "In sexual matters, the Jacobins thought and behaved (whatever their opponents claimed) like forerunners of the Evangelicals." Believing in the power of reason to liberate mankind, they renounced the example of "Rousseau, Goethe and Kotzebue . . . when they refused to exploit sexual passion as a powerful natural ally against a moribund society and its repressive conventions." Butler contrasts the English Jacobins unfavorably in this respect with their Continental counterparts, including Madame de Staël.

A feminist point of view is not only compatible with the argumentative style of an eighteenth-century moralist, but may be positively connected with it. Were *Mansfield Park* primarily about political and social questions *other* than feminist ones, the conservative character of the moral argument which it embodies would justify us in supposing it to be fundamentally conservative in outlook, but, if the feminist issues are the central ones, it may be that the orthodox, rather old-fashioned character of the argument indicates feminist radicalism rather than orthodoxy. An example may be useful here. In attacking the education commonly provided for middle-class girls, Mary Wollstonecraft says:

> Though moralists have agreed that the tenor of life seems to prove that *man* is prepared by various circumstances for a future state, they consistently concur in advising *woman* to provide only for the present.

She refers to the belief, best exemplified in Bishop Butler's *Analogy of*

Religion, and popularized in many sermons and moralistic works, that the world is so ordered as to teach us moral principle through secular experience. Even without a belief in God, the order of nature, including human nature, of which rational powers are a part, insures that we are rewarded when we act well and punished when we act badly. It was an orthodox belief of established moralists that this was so, but, in applying it to women, Mary Wollstonecraft is able to use it to attack existing practices in education and social custom, which rule out one half of mankind from the benefits of exercise in the moral gymnasium designed to teach moral principles.

In the Austen novels the heroines learn about morals through the application of rational reflection to experience. This is how they are shown to acquire principle. They never learn it from clerical advisers. The process by which they acquire understanding of duty, and of right courses of action, is entirely secular, as [Gilbert] Ryle noted. The way in which they are shown as becoming morally accountable may look a little old-fashioned, if we forget that they are young women, not young men. If we remember it, and see it in relation to contemporary feminist discussion, we may see that Jane Austen is sometimes a radical wolf when she pointedly adopts orthodox moralists' sheep's clothing.

It is time to return to Miss Fanny, and to show further that her characterization is to be illuminated by Mary Wollstonecraft. The implication of this must be that either Austen had read Wollstonecraft or that she was familiar with her works through the filtering through of their arguments and examples to other, less controversial writers. I do not mean to argue the case for direct influence here. During the five years she spent in Bath, with its well-stocked bookshops and circulating libraries, by no means confined to fiction, Austen had access to the works of Mary Wollstonecraft. In the absence of direct biographical information, the case must stand upon the probability implied by closeness of point of view and, in some instances, of allusion and vocabulary.

Vindication is not primarily about the political and constitutional rights of women, but about the ideas referred to above as constituting the essence of post-Enlightenment rational feminism. It is largely an attack upon Rousseau, especially the Rousseau of *Émile,* and upon those sentimental moralists and divines who had followed him in denying women the moral status of rational, adult, moral agents. With them are coupled imaginative writers of both sexes, including Madame de Staël, who, by emphasizing the sensibility of women at the expense of their powers of reason, have "Rendered them Objects of Pity, Bordering on Contempt." Wollstonecraft's animus against Rousseau arises from his having made Sophie—his ideal mate for

Émile, the ideal man—a different kind of moral creature. Whereas Émile is to enjoy bodily and mental exercise, Sophie is to be confined to bodily weakness and to obedience. This, Rousseau thought, was in accordance with the nature of the two sexes and with their purposes in life. It was for the man to enjoy the advantages of a free, experiential life; it was for the woman to please him, to arouse his sexual passion, to enjoy his protection, and to obey him. All this was anathema to Wollstonecraft and, to Austen, a fit subject of ridicule.

Take first the question of health and strength, which is of particular importance to the characterization of Miss Fanny. Wollstonecraft objects to Rousseau's belief that genuine weakness and the affected exaggeration of weakness are natural to women and a means by which they gain an ambiguous power over men. She quotes with disgust a passage from *Émile* in which it is asserted of women:

> So far from being ashamed of their weakness, they glory in it; their tender muscles make no resistance; they affect to be incapable of lifting the smallest burdens, and would blush to be thought robust and strong.

Wollstonecraft declares that

> the first care of mothers and fathers who really attend to the education of females should be, if not to strengthen the body, at least not to destroy the constitution by mistaken notions of female excellence; nor should girls ever be allowed to imbibe the pernicious notion that a defect can, by any chemical process of reasoning, become an excellence.

She then attacks such conduct-book authors as have taken their cue from Rousseau and encouraged girls to cultivate either real or affected weakness and low spirits. Among these she reluctantly places Dr. John Gregory, whose *A Father's Letters to His Daughters* (1774)

> actually recommends dissimulation and advises an innocent girl to give the lie to her feelings, and not dance with spirit, when gaiety of heart would make her feel eloquent without making her gestures immodest. In the name of truth and common sense, why should not one woman acknowledge that she has a better constitution than another?

Austen did not admire physical weakness or ill-health or ignorance in young women, but a lot of people, including those who ought to have known better, did. The relevance of this to Miss Price is obvious. Austen created in her a heroine whom the unwary might take for something like the Rousseauist ideal of the perfect woman, but she expects her more discerning readers to see through it, and gives them a good many indications that this is not a proper reading. The most important of these is, of course, the category mistake of the anti-hero, but there is a good deal else. The true hero is never shown as encouraging Fanny in her partly self-imposed fragility and timidity, although he is kind to her when he observes her genuine tendency to tire easily. He gets her a horse, encourages her to ride regularly, and tells her to speak up for herself, even to her uncle. But the major comic emphasis, through which Austen shows that she does not admire hypochondria in women, even beautiful ones, comes through the splendid portrait of pampered indolence in Lady Bertram.

Fanny is quite different from her aunt in that she has, both as a child and as a very vulnerable adolescent, experienced both neglect and hardship. Given Mrs. Price's predilection for sons and her slatternly housekeeping, there is little reason to think that the health (whether of body or mind) of her eldest daughter had ever received much attention. At Mansfield, the somnolence of Aunt Bertram, the sadism of Aunt Norris, and the false regard for wealth and status of Sir Thomas Bertram, his elder son, and his daughters, have all combined to ensure that Fanny's mental and physical health are put in jeopardy. She has not a strong constitution, but she was not as a child devoid of normal impulses to active life. She did not enjoy such freedom as Catherine Morland, rolling down green slopes with her brothers, and it is never positively established that she preferred cricket to dolls or nursing dormice, as Catherine did, but Fanny, in her early years at Portsmouth, was important as *"play-fellow,"* as well as "instructress and nurse" to her brothers and sisters. The single instance of remembered childhood activity which Austen mentions concerns dancing. William recalls how he and Fanny used to dance together as children. It is what prompts him to ask Sir Thomas if his sister is a good dancer, Sir Thomas being forced to reply that he does not know. William says, "I should like to be your partner once more. We used to jump about together many a time, did not we? when the hand organ was in the street?" Fanny's excessive fragility of body and lack of self-confidence are the result of inconsiderate, and sometimes humiliating, treatment by her illiberal, selfish aunts, but it has not quite stamped out of her an impulse to life which is to be seen in her continued love of dancing. At her first ball, "she was quite grieved to be losing even a quarter of an hour . . . sitting most unwillingly among the chaperons . . . while all the other young people were dancing." Later, when a ball is given in her honor, the narrator tells us, "She had hardly ever been in a state so nearly approaching high spirits in her life. Her cousins' former gaiety on the day of a ball was no longer surprising to her; she felt it to be indeed very charming." And she actually practices her steps in the drawing room, when she is sure Aunt Norris won't see. She gets tired later at this ball, partly because she is jealous of Miss Crawford, but it is three o'clock in the morning, and she is up earlier than anyone else, apart from William, next day, in order to see him off.

Fanny Price's feebleness is not a mark of Clarissa Harlowe-like saintliness, as Lionel Trilling thought, nor is it to be dismissed, as Marilyn Butler dismisses it, as "quite incidental." It is essential to the play of anti-Rousseauist, feminist irony upon Miss Price and those who seek to interpret her. Once her cousins leave Mansfield, prolonged ill-treatment is seen to have curious effects. The affectation of fragility, which it took an expensive education to achieve, Fanny lacks, but a genuine fragility now makes her seem something like the Rousseauist ideal, and by this Crawford is, as he puts it, "fairly caught." But, if Fanny's physical frailty amounts to more than it seems, the strength of her mind, despite the physical and emotional deprivation she has endured, is truly formidable. Housed within the "bewitching little body," lurking behind the "soft light eyes," is a clear, critical, rationally judging mind, quite unlike the tractable, childlike mind of the true conduct-book heroine. Wollstonecraft says, "The conduct of an accountable being must be regulated by the operation of its own reason; or on what foundation rests the throne of God?" (*Vindication*). Just before Fanny offends her uncle by insisting upon her right to regulate her conduct, by the operation of her own judgment, in a matter of great moment, he is made to say, though without understanding what it implies, "You have an understanding, which will prevent you from receiving things only in part, and judging partially by the event.—You will take in the whole of the past, you will consider times, persons, and probabilities." He is talking about Aunt Norris's past behavior, but he describes exactly what Fanny does in forming her opinion of Crawford.

The moral and comic climax of *Mansfield Park* occurs at the start of volume three, in the East room, when Fanny confronts her august uncle and defies him. Sir Thomas, once he is able to make out that she intends to refuse Crawford, thunders away at her about ingratitude, selfishness, perversity, and sheer obtuseness as to her own interest. He is forced to wonder if she does not show "that independence of spirit, which prevails so much in modern days, even in young women, and which in young women is offensive and disgusting beyond all common offence." Austen expects us to laugh at him, but she does not spare her heroine either. Returning from her walk in the shrubbery, Fanny finds that a fire has already been lighted, on Sir Thomas's orders, in the bleak East room. She does not day, as a creature wholly regulated by reason might have done, "Well, wrongly though he has judged and acted, he has kind and benevolent aspects." She says—and it is truer to life, as well as to the comic spirit— "in soliloquy," " 'I must be a brute indeed, if I can be really ungrateful. . . . Heaven defend me from being ungrateful.' "

Jane Austen laughs at Fanny when she herself acquiesces, as she often does, in the submissive role in which an unjust domestic "order" has cast her. She exposes, with a more bitter ridicule, the foolishness which has all but stamped out of Fanny her ability to laugh, dance, play, or to act—in any sense. But she does not despair. Reason, and the will of a less insane God than that invoked by such clerics as Fordyce and Mr. Collins or Dr. Grant, will prevail, where men have such sense as Edmund and women such sense as Fanny. "Good sense, like hers, will always act when really called upon," and so it does. Fanny becomes "the daughter that Sir Thomas Bertram wanted," that is, *lacked,* and, together with Edmund, is shown as capable of establishing at the parsonage a more liberal and more securely based domestic order than that of the Great House.

Fanny does not, as some critics, more concerned with mythic elements of plot than sound moral argument, have thought, "inherit" Mansfield Park. She marries the younger son, not the heir (who is pointedly restored to health), and she goes to live at the parsonage, where an enlightened, rational, secular Christianity is likely to be the order of the day. It is, perhaps, unlikely that the next Lady Bertram will waste so many years in a state of semiconsciousness, devoid of mental or physical life, upon a sofa, with a lapdog and a tangled, useless, meaningless bit of needlework, as the former Miss Maria Ward has done. But it is at the parsonage, not the Great House, that there is to occur that "unspeakable gain in private happiness to the liberated half of the species; the difference to them between a life of subjection to the will of others, and a life of rational freedom," of which J. S. Mill was later to write.

In *Mansfield Park,* Austen shows some sympathy with points made in the *Vindication* and anticipates Mill *On the Subjection of Women.* It looks to me as though she may also have profited from a critical reading of Woll-stonecraft's two novels. There is no direct evidence that she read them, but Godwin's publication of his *Memoirs of the Author of a Vindication of the Rights of Woman* in 1798 caused a great deal of interest in its subject. The "Advertisement" to *Mary* (1788) tells us that its heroine is "neither a Clarissa, a Lady G. [randison] nor a Sophie." In it, "the mind of a woman who has thinking powers" is to be displayed. Mary, its heroine, had "read Butler's *Analogy,* and some other authors: and these researches made her a Christian from conviction." Austen would not have countenanced the pretentious tone of this, but, in her own ironic way, she shows us that much the same could be said of Fanny. By the time *Maria* was written—it was still unfinished in 1797, when Wollstonecraft died—the author had become a Deist, rather than a Christian, but this does not prevent her from applying Butler's argument about how we learn moral principles in her new work. She says that in most novels "the hero is allowed to be mortal, and to become wise and virtuous as well as happy, by a train of events and circumstances. The heroines, on the contrary, are to be born immaculate."

Both in Wollstonecraft and Austen, the language of law and property as well as the language of capture and captivation are shown as improperly applied to marriage and to decent sexual relationships. *Mansfield Park* opens with the *captivation* by Miss *Ward* of *Huntingdon*, of a baronet to whom her uncle, *"the lawyer, himself,* . . . allowed her to be at least three thousand pounds short of any *equitable claim"* (my italics). Wollstonecraft's Maria talks about "the master key of property." Austen, in the Sotherton episode, makes use of the lock and key image in connection with Rushworth and his property. Wollstonecraft's Maria says, "Marriage had bastilled me for life." Maria Bertram, flirting with Crawford while her intended husband has gone off to look for the key to the iron gate, which gives her "a feeling of restraint and hardship," alludes to the starling which Yorick found caged in the Bastille, and which sang incessantly, "I can't get out, I can't get out." She also refers to Sotherton as a prison, "quite a dismal old prison." Wollstonecraft's anti-hero declares "that every woman has her price." Austen borrows, as the name for her heroine, that of Crabbe's in one of *The Parish Register* tales. Crabbe's Fanny Price is a refuser of the captive-captivate game; Austen's is shown as unfit, by her nature, to become a commodity in the marriage market, though capable of paying the price of enduring wrongful abuse and misunderstanding, which secures her "right to choose, like the rest of us."

Jane Austen does not, like Mary Wollstonecraft, present us with an innocent heroine imprisoned in a marriage for which she is not regarded as bearing a responsibility. Austen's Maria chooses her own fate, though neither Sir Thomas nor the moral standards of the society of which he is a pillar are held blameless. Fanny, who avoids an imprisoning marriage, since she enters a partnership based on affection and esteem, does so not because she is "innocent," but because she is what Milton called [in

Areopagitica] "a true wayfaring Christian." Hers is not "a fugitive and cloistered virtue, unexercised and unbreathed," but one that has been put to "trial . . . by what is contrary."

Once the irony at work in the characterization of Miss Price is recognized, the way is open to consideration of what is shown as truly valuable in the right ordering of domestic society and in the world beyond it. Jane Austen did not believe that individuals had to create their own morality; she believed that moral law was objectively enshrined in the nature of the world itself. To that extent, she supposes that human beings are required to be obedient to moral laws or principles, but she is perfectly clear that the individual human being has the right, and duty, of determining, by the operation of his or her own reason, what these principles are and how they are to be applied in the personal regulation of conduct. By showing that Sir Thomas's niece and his younger son are better to be relied upon in judging correctly, an implicit criticism of "birthright and habit," which debar women and younger sons from influence, even when their superior abilities are known, is made. It is quite in line with Wollstonecraft's attitude to "the Pernicious Effects which Arise from the Unnatural Distinctions Established in Society" (part of the title of chapter 9 of *Vindication*). When Mary Crawford says that Edmund ought to have gone into Parliament, he replies, "I believe I must wait till there is an especial assembly for the representation of younger sons who have little to live on." Sir Thomas is a Member of Parliament, as, presumably, his elder son will also be. It is suggested that Mr. Rushworth will also enter the House when Sir Thomas is able to find him a borough. A rotten borough is not specified but would undoubtedly be appropriate. The case for the recognition of the *equality* of women with men is implicitly allied with the case against such unnatural distinctions and inequalities as are inherent in the law of primogeniture and in the unrepresentative character of Parliament.

Mansfield Park is also pointedly concerned with *fraternity*. What ought to be, and sometimes is—as in the relationship between Fanny and her brother William—the paradigm of equal, affectionate relationships between men and women is always held up as an ideal, having implications beyond the literal meaning of "brother" and "sister." Edmund Bertram treats his inferior little cousin as a sister early in volume 1. He does not fall in love with her until the final chapter, in which this is treated cursorily and ironically. This is not because Jane Austen had suddenly and unselfconsciously become interested in incest; it is because the marriage which provides the necessary happy ending of a comic work carries implications about the right relationships between men and women, both in marriage as a social institution and in society at large. As Mill was to say some fifty or more years later:

> The moral regeneration of mankind will only really commence, when the most fundamental of the social relations is placed under the rule of equal justice, and when human beings learn to cultivate their strongest sympathy with an equal in rights and cultivation.

Austen, in *Mansfield Park,* shows that such an ideal is more readily to be found, in contemporary society, between brothers and sisters than husbands and wives, though she seeks a transference to the marriage relationship of the ideal. With William, Fanny experiences a "felicity" which she has never known before, in an "unchecked, equal, fearless intercourse."

It is, however, with liberty, and the moral basis upon which individual liberty must be founded, that *Mansfield Park* is clearest and boldest. Women, in the Midland counties of England, like servants, were not slaves. Even a *wife,* not beloved, had some protection, "in the laws of the land, and the manners of the age." So Catherine Morland had learnt, under the tutelage of Henry Tilney. "Murder was not tolerated . . . and neither poison nor sleeping potions to be procured like rhubarb, from every druggist" (*Northanger Abbey*). But what of an indulged wife? And a falsely respected one? In the Midland counties of England, murder might not be necessary where a wife could retain all the advantages of outward respect, rank, precedence, and "respectability," while passing her days in a state of partly self-induced semiconsciousness. Lady Bertram had "been a beauty, and a prosperous beauty, all her life; and beauty and wealth were all that excited her respect." She values herself on her possession of these things and, in the corrupt social order of which she is part, is valued for them. Never shown as going outside, or breathing fresh English air, Lady Bertram represents the slavery to which women who accede to such ideas reduce themselves, with the unwitting connivance of those, like Sir Thomas, who see nothing disgraceful in their condition. Not literally a slave and not suffering from the effects of a literal sleeping potion, what is she as a human being? What is she morally, as a rational, accountable one?

It is well known that in America the movement for women's rights was accelerated by the part women played in the movement for the emancipation of the slaves. As they heard, and put, moral arguments against slavery, they made an analogy between the moral status of a slave and of a woman, especially a married woman. This analogy is made in the *Vindication* and implied in *Mansfield Park*. Wollstonecraft says that a "truly benevolent legislator always endeavours to make it the interest of each individual to be virtuous; and thus private virtue becoming the cement of public happiness, an orderly whole is consolidated by the tendency of all the parts towards a common centre." Women, however, are not taught to be virtuous in their domestic life and so are not to be trusted in either private or public life. They learn to be subject to propriety, "blind propriety," rather than to regulate their actions in accordance with moral law as "an heir of immortality" ought. She asks, "Is one half of the human species, like the poor African slaves, to be subjected to prejudices that brutalise them, when principles would be a surer guard of virtue?"

In England, agitation against the slave trade had gone on all through the last quarter of the eighteenth century. The arguments against it were rehearsed widely in the early nineteenth century, leading up to the passing of the Act of Abolition, which became effective in 1808. Jane Austen must have been familiar with them and, in a letter of 1813, speaks of having been in love with Thomas Clarkson's writings. In 1808, Clarkson published *The Abolition of the African Slave Trade:*

> We have lived in consequence of it to see the day when it has been recorded as a principle of our legislation that commerce itself shall have its moral boundaries. We have lived to see the day when we are likely to be delivered from the contagion of the most barbarous opinions. Those who supported this wicked traffic virtually denied that man was a moral being. They substituted the law of force for the law of reason. But the great Act, now under our consideration, had banished the impious doctrine and restored the rational creature to his moral rights.

It is easy to see here that a woman who rejoiced that the slave trade had been ended might ask whether it had yet been recorded "as a principle of our legislation that commerce itself shall have its moral boundaries"—so far as women were concerned. Was it universally accepted that woman was "a moral being"? Had the rational creature been restored to *her* moral rights?

Clarkson goes over the history of the anti-slavery movement and refers to a particularly famous legal judgment, which established that slavery was illegal in England. This was the Mansfield Judgment, given by the Lord Chief Justice of England in 1772, in a case concerning a black slave, James Somerset, the question being whether, having been brought to England, he could still be held to be "owned" by his master. Arguing that he could not, counsel for the defence, referring to an earlier judgment given in the reign of Queen Elizabeth, said:

it was resolved that England was too pure an air for slaves to breathe in . . . and I hope my lord the air does not blow worse since—I hope they will never breathe here; for this is my assertion, the moment they put their feet on English ground, that moment they are free.

Lord Mansfield found in favor of Somerset and, by implication, of this view of English air.

In *Mansfield Park* the English patriarch is also the owner of Antiguan plantations and of the slaves who work them. When he returns to England, his niece puts a question to him about the slave trade. We are not told what the question was, nor what answer was given, but, through her title, the making of Sir Thomas a slaveowner abroad, and the unstated question of Miss Fanny, *her* moral status in England is implicitly contrasted, yet also compared, with that of the Antiguan slaves. Since it is often assumed that Jane Austen could not have thought much about anything which did not impinge upon her domestic life and familial relations, or else been said by Dr. Johnson, it may be worth noting that at the house of her brother Edward she met Lord Mansfield's niece on a number of occasions, and that Boswell reported Johnson's view on another slavery case, *Knight* v. *Wedderburn,* as follows: "No man is by nature the property of another. The defendant is therefore by nature free!"

Slaves have masters but cannot truly be said to have a country, since they are neither protected by its laws nor accorded those rights which belong to freeborn citizens. That this was true in England of women is a point made by Wollstonecraft in *Maria,* where the heroine has no redress in "the laws of her country—if women have a country." Austen, not doubting that even such an unpromising feminist as Fanny Price "speaks the tongue that Shakespeare spoke" and, apart, no doubt, from a small difference about Adam and Eve, holds "the faith and morals . . . which Milton held," assumes that enlightened readers will know that she has the same "titles manifold" to British freedom as anyone else. She assures us that the soil at Mansfield is good, especially at the parsonage, and she makes a great point of the wholesomeness of English air, which is frequently associated with health and liberty. At Sotherton, with its prisonlike atmosphere, all the young people share "one impulse, one wish for air and liberty." Fanny's need for fresh English air is stressed again and again, often in ironic contexts. After berating her for not accepting Crawford, Sir Thomas tells her to get some exercise outside, where "the air will do her good," and Henry Crawford says of her, that she "requires constant air and exercise . . . ought never to be long banished from the free air and liberty of the country." Of course, he means the countryside, but does not Austen expect the intelligent, enlightened reader to see a bit further?

Finally, we come to *Lovers' Vows*. It has been thought that, because this play had been attacked in anti-Jacobin circles, Austen's choice of it must be taken as a sign of her reactionary political viewpoint. However, it is quite directly associated with the main feminist themes of this novel. For a start, as its title shows, it is about the sentimental treatment of lovers' promises and is used to point the contrast between the lack of commitment involved in such promises as Baron Wildenhaim made to Agatha before he seduced her, or as Crawford half-makes to Maria, and the binding nature of the marriage contract. *Lovers' Vows* is a work in that tradition of Rousseauist literature which Mary Wollstonecraft objected to as rendering women objects of pity bordering on contempt. Agatha, having endured twenty years of poverty and humiliation because Wildenhaim broke his promise to her, makes a grateful, tearful acceptance of his eventual offer (following their son's intervention) to marry him. The curtain comes down on the following tableau:

> Anhalt leads on Agatha—The Baron runs and clasps her in his arms—supported by him, she sinks on a chair which Amelia places in the middle of the stage—The Baron kneels by her side, holding her hand.
> BARON. Agatha, Agatha, do you know this voice?
> AGATHA. Wildenhaim.
> BARON. Can you forgive me?
> AGATHA. I forgive you (*embracing him*).
> FREDERICK (*as he enters*). I hear the voice of my mother!—Ha! mother! father!
> (Frederick throws himself on his knees by the other side of his mother—She clasps him in her arms.—Amelia is placed on the side of her father attentively viewing Agatha—Anhalt stands on the side of Frederick with his hands gratefully raised to Heaven.)
> The curtain slowly drops.

Anyone who doubts whether Jane Austen laughed at this had better reread *Love and Freindship*, but we have good reason to suppose that she thought the "happy ending" morally objectionable, not because the baron was letting his class down by marrying a village girl, nor the honor of his sex by marrying the girl who had lost her virtue through his agency, but because Agatha should have had more respect for herself, and too much contempt for him to have him at any price.

Mansfield Park remains a puzzling novel, partly, I think, because Jane Austen enjoyed puzzles and thought it both amusing and instructive to solve them. She asks a great deal of her readers—sound moral attitudes, derived from rational reflection upon experience; quick-wittedness and ingenuity in making connections; and a belief in the wholesomeness of laughter. It would be possible to make of *Mansfield Park* something like a piece of feminist propaganda, in which regulated hatred predominates, but it would be false. It is a great comic novel, regulated by the sane laughter of an impish, rational feminist. The pricelessness of Miss Price is its heart—and head.

Chronology

<table>
<tr><td>1775</td><td>Jane Austen is born on December 16 in the village of Steventon, Hampshire, to George Austen, parish clergyman, and Cassandra Leigh Austen. She is the seventh of eight children. She and her sister Cassandra are educated at Oxford and Southampton by the widow of a Principal of Brasenose College, and then attend the Abbey School at Reading. Jane's formal education ends when she is nine years old.</td></tr>
<tr><td>1787–93</td><td>Austen writes various pieces for the amusement of her family (now collected in the three volumes of *Juvenilia*), the most famous of which is *Love and Freindship*. She and her family also perform in the family barn various plays and farces, some of which are written by Jane.</td></tr>
<tr><td>1793–95</td><td>Austen writes her first novel, the epistolary *Lady Susan,* and begins the epistolary *Elinor and Marianne,* which will become *Sense and Sensibility.*</td></tr>
<tr><td>1796–97</td><td>Austen completes *First Impressions,* an early version of *Pride and Prejudice.* Her father tries to get it published without success. Austen begins *Sense and Sensibility* and *Northanger Abbey.*</td></tr>
<tr><td>1798</td><td>Austen finishes a version of *Northanger Abbey.*</td></tr>
<tr><td>1801</td><td>George Austen retires to Bath with his family.</td></tr>
<tr><td>1801–2</td><td>Jane Austen probably suffers from an unhappy love affair (the man in question is believed to have died suddenly) and also probably becomes engaged for a day to Harris Bigg-Wither.</td></tr>
<tr><td>1803</td><td>Austen sells a two-volume manuscript entitled *Susan* to a publisher for £10. It is advertised, but never printed. This is a version of *Northanger Abbey,* probably later revised.</td></tr>
<tr><td>1803–5</td><td>Austen writes ten chapters of *The Watsons,* which is never finished.</td></tr>
<tr><td>1805</td><td>George Austen dies. Jane abandons work on *The Watsons.*</td></tr>
</table>

1805–6   Jane Austen, her mother, and her sister live in various lodgings in Bath.

1806–9   The three Austen women move to Southampton, living near one of Jane's brothers.

1809   The three Austen women move to Chawton Cottage, in Hampshire, which is part of the estate of Jane's brother Edward Austen (later Knight), who has been adopted by Thomas Knight, a relative. Edward has just lost his wife, who died giving birth to her tenth child, and the household has been taken over by Jane's favorite niece, Fanny.

1811   Austen decides to publish *Sense and Sensibility* at her own expense and anonymously. It comes out in November, in three volumes.

1811–12   Austen is probably revising *First Impressions* extensively, and beginning *Mansfield Park*.

1813   *Pride and Prejudice: A Novel. In Three Volumes. By the Author of 'Sense and Sensibility'* is published in January. Second editions of both books come out in November.

1814   *Mansfield Park* is published, again anonymously, and in three volumes. It sells out by November. Austen begins *Emma*.

1815   Austen finishes *Emma,* and begins *Persuasion. Emma* is published in December, anonymously, in three volumes, by a new publisher.

1816   A second edition of *Mansfield Park* is published.

1817   A third edition of *Pride and Prejudice* is published. Austen begins *Sanditon*. She moves to Winchester, where she dies, after a year-long illness, on July 18. She is buried in Winchester Cathedral. After her death, her family destroys much of her correspondence, in order to protect her reputation.

1818   *Persuasion* and *Northanger Abbey* are published posthumously together; their authorship is still officially anonymous.

Contributors

HAROLD BLOOM, Sterling Professor of the Humanities at Yale University, is the author of *The Anxiety of Influence, Poetry and Repression,* and many other volumes of literary criticism. His forthcoming study, *Freud: Transference and Authority,* attempts a full-scale reading of all of Freud's major writings. A MacArthur Prize Fellow, he is general editor of five series of literary criticism published by Chelsea House.

THOMAS R. EDWARDS is Professor of English at Rutgers University. He is the author of *This Dark Estate,* a reading of Alexander Pope's poetry, and of several studies of the relation of poetry to politics.

ALISTAIR M. DUCKWORTH is Professor of English at the University of Florida, Gainesville. He is the author of *The Improvement of the Estate: A Study of Jane Austen's Novels.*

STUART M. TAVE is William Rainey Harper Professor in the College and Professor of English at The University of Chicago. His books include *Some Words of Jane Austen, New Essays by De Quincey,* and a study of comic theory and criticism in the eighteenth and nineteenth centuries.

JULIET MCMASTER is Professor of English at the University of Alberta. She is the author of *Thackeray: The Major Novels, Trollope's Palliser Novels: Theme and Pattern,* and *Jane Austen on Love.*

SUSAN MORGAN is Assistant Professor of English at Stanford University and the author of *In the Meantime: Character and Perception in Jane Austen's Fiction.*

DAVID MONAGHAN is Professor of English at Mount Saint Vincent University in Halifax, Nova Scotia. He is the editor of *Jane Austen in a Social Context* and the author of *Jane Austen: Structure and Social Vision* and *The Novels of John Le Carré.*

137

NINA AUERBACH is Associate Professor of English at the University of Pennsylvania. She is the author of *Communities of Women: An Idea in Fiction* and *Woman and the Demon: The Life of a Victorian Myth.*

MARGARET KIRKHAM teaches at Bristol Polytechnic and is the author of *Jane Austen: Feminism and Fiction.*

Bibliography

Babb, Howard. *Jane Austen's Novels: The Fabric of Dialogue*. Columbus: Ohio State University Press, 1962.

Banfield, Ann. "The Moral Landscape of *Mansfield Park*." *Nineteenth-Century Fiction* 26 (1971): 1–24.

Bowen, Elizabeth. "Jane Austen." In *The English Novelists,* edited by Derek Verschoyle, 101–13. New York: Harcourt, Brace & Co., 1936.

Bradbrook, Frank. *Jane Austen and Her Predecessors*. Cambridge: Cambridge University Press, 1967.

Bradbrook, M. C. "A Note on Fanny Price." *Essays in Criticism* 5 (1955): 289–92.

Branton, C. L. "The Ordinations in Jane Austen's Novels." *Nineteenth-Century Fiction* 10 (1955): 156–59.

Brown, Julia Prewitt. *Jane Austen's Novels: Social Change and Literary Form*. Cambridge: Harvard University Press, 1979.

Brown, Lloyd. *Bits of Ivory: Narrative Techniques in Jane Austen's Fiction*. Baton Rouge: Louisiana State University Press, 1973.

Burroway, Janet. "The Irony of the Insufferable Prig: *Mansfield Park*." *Critical Quarterly* 9 (1967): 127–38.

Bush, Douglas. *Jane Austen*. New York: Macmillan, 1975.

Butler, Marilyn. *Jane Austen and the War of Ideas*. Oxford: Oxford University Press, 1975.

Carroll, David R. "*Mansfield Park, Daniel Deronda,* and Ordination." *Modern Philology* 62 (1965): 217–26.

Cecil, David. *A Portrait of Jane Austen*. New York: Hill & Wang, 1980.

Chabot, C. Barry. "Jane Austen's Novels: The Vicissitudes of Desire." *American Imago* 32 (1975): 288–308.

Chapman, R. W. *Jane Austen: Facts and Problems*. Oxford: Clarendon Press, 1948.

Colby, R. A. *Fiction with a Purpose*. Bloomington: Indiana University Press, 1967.

Collins, Barbara B. "Jane Austen's Victorian Novel." *Nineteenth-Century Fiction* 4 (1949): 175–85.

Cowart, David. "Wise and Foolish Virgins (and Matrons) in *Mansfield Park*." *South Atlantic Bulletin* 44, no. 2 (1979): 76–82.

Craik, W. A. *Jane Austen: The Six Novels*. London: Methuen, 1966.

DeRose, Peter. "Hardship, Recollection, and Discipline: Three Lessons in *Mansfield Park*." *Studies in the Novel* 9 (1977): 261–78.

Devlin, David. *Jane Austen and Education*. New York: Barnes & Noble Books, 1975.
———. "*Mansfield Park*." *Ariel* 2 (1971): 30–44.
Donohue, Joseph W., Jr. "Ordination and the Divided House at Mansfield Park." *ELH* 32, no. 2 (1965): 169–78.
Donovan, Robert. *The Shaping Vision: Imagination in the English Novel from Defoe to Dickens*. Ithaca, N.Y.: Cornell University Press, 1966.
Draffan, R. A. "*Mansfield Park:* Jane Austen's Bleak House." *Essays in Criticism* 19 (1969): 371–84.
Duffy, Joseph M., Jr. "Moral Integrity and Moral Anarchy in *Mansfield Park*." *ELH* 23 (1956): 71–91.
Edge, C. E. "*Mansfield Park* and Ordination." *Nineteenth-Century Fiction* 16 (1961): 269–74.
Fergus, Jan. *Jane Austen and the Didactic Novel:* Northanger Abbey, Sense and Sensibility, *and* Pride and Prejudice. Totowa, N.J.: Barnes & Noble Books, 1983.
Fleishman, Avrom. *A Reading of* Mansfield Park: *An Essay in Critical Synthesis*. Minneapolis: University of Minnesota Press, 1967.
Giuffre, Giula. "Sex, Self, and Society in *Mansfield Park*." *Sydney Studies in English* 9 (1983–84): 76–93.
Gould, Gerald. "The Gate Scene at Sotherton in *Mansfield Park*." *Literature and Psychology* 20 (1970): 75–78.
Grove, Robin. "Jane Austen's Free Enquiry: *Mansfield Park*." *The Critical Review* 25 (1983): 132–50.
Gullans, C. B. "Jane Austen's *Mansfield Park* and Dr. Johnson." *Nineteenth-Century Fiction* 27 (1972): 206–8.
Halperin, John. *The Life of Jane Austen*. Sussex: Harvester Press, 1984.
———, ed. *Jane Austen: Bicentenary Essays*. Cambridge: Cambridge University Press, 1975.
Hardy, Barbara. *A Reading of Jane Austen*. New York: New York University Press, 1976.
Hardy, John. *Jane Austen's Heroines: Intimacy in Human Relationships*. London: Routledge & Kegan Paul, 1984.
Heath, William, ed. *Discussions of Jane Austen*. Boston: D. C. Heath & Co., 1961.
Hummel, Madeline. "Emblematic Charades and the Observant Woman in *Mansfield Park*." *Texas Studies in Literature and Language* 15 (1973): 251–66.
Jones, Myrddin. "Feelings of Youth and Nature in *Mansfield Park*." *English* 29, no. 135 (1980): 221–32.
Kelly, Gary. "Reading Aloud in *Mansfield Park*." *Nineteenth-Century Fiction* 37, no. 1 (1982): 29–50.
Kirkham, Margaret. *Jane Austen: Feminism and Fiction*. Totowa, N.J.: Barnes & Noble Books, 1983.
Koppel, Gene. "The Role of Contingency in *Mansfield Park:* The Necessity of an Ambiguous Conclusion." *Southern Review* (Adelaide) 15, no. 3 (1982): 306–13.
Kroeber, Karl. *Styles in Fictional Structure: The Art of Jane Austen, Charlotte Brontë, George Eliot*. Princeton: Princeton University Press, 1971.
Lascelles, Mary. *Jane Austen and Her Art*. Oxford: Oxford University Press, 1939.
Lenta, Margaret. "Androgyny and Authority in *Mansfield Park*." *Studies in the Novel* 15, no. 3 (1983): 169–82.

Lerner, Laurence. *The Truthtellers: Jane Austen, George Eliot, D. H. Lawrence.* New York: Schocken Books, 1967.

Liddell, Robert. *Novels of Jane Austen.* London: Longmans, Green & Co., 1963.

Litz, A. Walton. *Jane Austen: A Study of Her Artistic Development.* New York: Oxford University Press, 1965.

Lodge, David. "A Question of Judgment: The Theatricals at Mansfield Park." *Nineteenth-Century Fiction* 17 (1962): 275–82.

McMaster, Juliet. *Jane Austen on Love.* Victoria, B.C.: University of Victoria Press, 1978.

———, ed. *Jane Austen's Achievement.* London: Macmillan, 1976.

Mansell, Darrel. *The Novels of Jane Austen: An Interpretation.* London: Macmillan, 1973.

Mews, Hazel. *Frail Vessels: Woman's Role in Women's Novels from Fanny Burney to George Eliot.* London: Athlone Press, 1969.

Moler, Kenneth L. *Jane Austen's Art of Illusion.* Lincoln: University of Nebraska Press, 1968.

———. " 'Only Connect': Emotional Strength and Health in *Mansfield Park.*" *English Studies* 64, no. 2 (1983): 144–52.

Monaghan, David. *Jane Austen: Structure and Social Vision.* London: Macmillan, 1980.

———, ed. *Jane Austen in a Social Context.* London: Macmillan, 1981.

Moore, Susan. "The Heroine of *Mansfield Park.*" *English Studies* 63, no. 2 (1982): 139–44.

Mudrick, Marvin. *Jane Austen: Irony as Defense and Discovery.* Princeton: Princeton University Press, 1952.

Nardin, Jane. *Those Elegant Decorums: The Concept of Propriety in Jane Austen's Novels.* Albany: State University of New York Press, 1973.

Nineteenth-Century Fiction 30, no. 3 (December 1975). Special Jane Austen issue.

Odmark, John. *An Understanding of Jane Austen's Novels.* Oxford: Basil Blackwell, 1981.

O'Neill, Judith. *Critics on Jane Austen.* Miami, Fla.: University of Miami Press, 1970.

Page, Norman. *The Language of Jane Austen.* Oxford: Basil Blackwell, 1972.

Paris, Bernard. *Character and Conflict in Jane Austen's Novels.* Detroit: Wayne State University Press, 1979.

Patterson, Emily H. "Family and Pilgrimage Themes in Austen's *Mansfield Park.*" *CLA Journal* 20, no. 1 (1976): 14–18.

Person, Leland S., Jr. "Playing House: Jane Austen's Fabulous Space." *Philological Quarterly* 59, no. 1 (1980): 62–75.

Persuasions: Journal of the Jane Austen Society of North America, 1979–.

Phillips, K. C. *Jane Austen's English.* London: Andre Deutsch Ltd., 1970.

Piggott, Patrick. *The Innocent Diversion: A Study of Music in the Life and Writings of Jane Austen.* London: Douglas Cleverdon, 1979.

Polhemus, Robert. *Comic Faith: The Great Tradition from Austen to Joyce.* Chicago: University of Chicago Press, 1980.

Poovey, Mary. *The Proper Lady and the Woman Writer: Ideology as Style in the Works of Mary Wollstonecraft, Mary Shelley, and Jane Austen.* Chicago: University of Chicago Press, 1984.

Ram, Atma. "Frail and Weak: A Portrait of Fanny Price." *Punjab University Research Bulletin* 8, nos. 1–2 (1977): 27–34.

Rees, Joan. *Jane Austen: Woman and Writer*. New York: St. Martin's Press, 1976.

Roberts, Warren. *Jane Austen and the French Revolution*. New York: St. Martin's Press, 1979.

Roth, Barry and Joel Weinsheimer, eds. *An Annotated Bibliography of Jane Austen Studies, 1952–1972*. Charlottesville: University Press of Virginia, 1973.

Ruoff, Gene W. "The Sense of a Beginning: *Mansfield Park*." *The Wordsworth Circle* 10, no. 2 (1979): 174–86.

Ryals, Clyde. "Being and Doing in *Mansfield Park*." *Archiv* 206 (1970): 345–60.

Scott, P. J. M. *Jane Austen: A Reassessment*. Totowa, N.J.: Barnes & Noble Books, 1982.

Sherry, Norman. *Jane Austen*. London: Evans Brothers, 1966.

Smith, LeRoy W. *Jane Austen and the Drama of Woman*. London: Macmillan & Co., 1983.

Southam, B. C. *Jane Austen*. Essex: Longman Group Ltd., 1975.

———, ed. *Critical Essays on Jane Austen*. London: Routledge & Kegan Paul, 1968.

———, ed. *Jane Austen: The Critical Heritage*. London: Routledge & Kegan Paul, 1968.

Steeves, Harrison. *Before Jane Austen*. New York: Holt, Rinehart & Winston, 1965.

Studies in the Novel 7, no. 1 (1975). Special Jane Austen issue.

Tanner, Tony. Introduction to *Mansfield Park*. Baltimore: Penguin Books, 1966.

Ten Harmsel, Henrietta. *Jane Austen: A Study in Fictional Conventions*. The Hague: Mouton & Co., 1964.

Todd, Janet, ed. *Jane Austen: New Perspectives. Women & Literature,* n.s. 3. New York: Holmes & Meier, 1983.

Watt, Ian. *Jane Austen: A Collection of Essays*. Englewood Cliffs, N.J.: Prentice-Hall, 1963.

Weinsheimer, Joel, ed. *Jane Austen Today*. Athens: The University of Georgia Press, 1975.

White, E. M. "A Critical Theory of *Mansfield Park*." *Studies in English Literature 1500–1900* 7 (1967): 659–77.

Wiesenfarth, Joseph. *The Errand of Form*. New York: Fordham University Press, 1967.

Wilson, Mona. *Jane Austen and Some Contemporaries*. London: Cresset Press, 1938.

The Wordsworth Circle 7, no. 4 (1976). Special Jane Austen issue.

Wright, Andrew. *Jane Austen's Novels: A Study in Structure*. New York: Oxford University Press, 1953.

Zelicovici, Dvora. "The Inefficacy of *Lovers' Vows*." *ELH* 50, no. 3 (1983): 531–40.

Zimmerman, Everett. "Jane Austen and *Mansfield Park*: A Discrimination of Ironies." *Studies in the Novel* 1 (1969): 347–56.

Acknowledgments

"The Difficult Beauty of *Mansfield Park*" by Thomas R. Edwards, Jr. from *Nineteenth-Century Fiction* 20, no. 1 (June 1965), © 1965 by the Regents of the University of California. Reprinted by permission of the University of California Press.

"The Improvement of the Estate" (originally entitled "*Mansfield Park:* Jane Austen's Grounds of Being") by Alistair M. Duckworth from *The Improvement of the Estate: A Study of Jane Austen's Novels* by Alistair M. Duckworth, © 1971 by The Johns Hopkins University Press. Reprinted by permission.

"Propriety and *Lovers' Vows*" (originally entitled "Fanny Price") by Stuart M. Tave from *Some Words of Jane Austen* by Stuart M. Tave, © 1973 by The University of Chicago. Reprinted by permission of The University of Chicago Press.

"Love: Surface and Subsurface" (originally entitled "Surface and Subsurface") by Juliet McMaster from *Jane Austen on Love* (English Literary Studies, no. 13) by Juliet McMaster, © 1978 by Juliet McMaster. Reprinted by permission. This essay was first published in *Ariel* 5, no. 2 (1974). © 1974 by the Board of Governors, the University of Calgary.

"The Promise of *Mansfield Park*" by Susan Morgan from *In the Meantime: Character and Perception in Jane Austen's Fiction* by Susan Morgan, © 1980 by The University of Chicago. Reprinted by permission of The University of Chicago Press.

"Structure and Social Vision" (originally entitled "*Mansfield Park*") by David Monaghan from *Jane Austen: Structure and Social Vision* by David Monaghan, © 1980 by David Monaghan. Reprinted by permission of the author and Macmillan, London and Basingstoke.

"Feeling as One Ought about Fanny Price" (originally entitled "Jane Austen's Dangerous Charm: Feeling as One Ought about Fanny Price") by Nina Auerbach from *Jane Austen: New Perspectives* (*Women and Literature,* n.s. 3), edited by Janet Todd, © 1983 by Holmes & Meier Publishers, Inc. Reprinted by permission.

"Feminist Irony and the Priceless Heroine of *Mansfield Park*" by Margaret Kirkham from *Jane Austen: New Perspectives* (*Women and Literature*, n.s. 3), edited by Janet Todd, © 1983 by Holmes & Meier Publishers, Inc. Reprinted by permission.

Index of Names and Titles